Patricia Coulter

Like Leaven

Accompanying Children on their Spiritual Journey

Amor Deus Publishing

Like Leaven
Accompanying Children on their Spiritual Journey
Patricia Coulter

Copyright © 2014, Patricia Coulter. All rights reserved.

Cover Photo: Sophia Cavalletti with a young boy in the Atrium by Douglas R. Gilbert
Cover image: Shutterstock
Cover and book design: Amor Deus Design Department

No part of this book may be reproduced, stored in a retrieval system or transmitted in any form or by any means - electronic, mechanical, photocopying, recording, or otherwise - without written permission of the publisher.

For information regarding permission, write to:
Amor Deus Publishing
Attention: Permissions Dept.
4727 North 12th Street
Phoenix, AZ 85014

ISBN 978-1-61956-255-4

First Edition September 2014
10 9 8 7 6 5 4 3 2 1

Printed in the United States of America by Amor Deus Publishing, an imprint of Vesuvius Press Incorporated.

♻ Text printed on 30% post-consumer waste recycled paper.

Visit us at AmorDeus.com

Dedication

The first is the moment of falling in love;
it is the attraction to the light.

—Sofia Cavalletti
Way of Holy Joy

In Memoriam

Sofia Cavalletti

Tilde Cocchini

Gianna Gobbi

Valentina Lillig

Dalmazio Mongillo, O.P.

Foreword

There are some moments in life that we look back upon and realize they were turning points in our journey through life. In 1978 I was sitting in a class at the University of St. Michael's taking what they called an "intersession course". I was working on a theology degree and saw this course as a way to pick up another credit and move closer to completing my course work. Sofia Cavalletti was talking about catechesis with young children and, as a school teacher, I hoped her course would be of some practical value to me when I returned to teaching. After a few rather typical classes, we arrived one day to find young kids in the classroom, perhaps about 10 of them. Sofia then proceeded to teach the children. It was pretty clear from the outset that these were not particularly "religious" kids and I waited patiently to see how long it would be before their attention wandered away from the "religion lesson" and their behaviour became problematic. Sofia was seated at floor level with the children and she seemed to not notice that we, the budding theologians carrying the heavy tomes and thinking the great ideas, were all around her. In very short order, the children also seemed unaware of us as they focused on and entered into the activities of the lesson. It was a real model lesson, better than anything I had observed during teacher training. Here was a teacher dealing directly with children and not simply talking about how to deal with children. Impressed was I!

After the children departed, one of Sofia's catechists then led a reflection on the Lost Sheep parable and had each of us take a turn down on the floor as she manipulated little wooden figures of sheep and a shepherd. Yawn, kid's stuff, no depth of theological insight, no over-arching themes. Then it happened and it has never left my consciousness—it's like it occurred just today. Somehow, I was directly with those sheep, looking to that shepherd as one who cared deeply for me; I felt the security of the gate that enclosed the flock; I was so happy. But wait, one of us is missing, one of us has wandered away! Well, you know the rest of the story.

So what about a "turning point"? A genuine interest in theology and a rather robust Catholic life-style suddenly morphed into a direct encounter with the Lord. When I returned to my seat, everything seemed different. My knowledge of the faith and my religious understanding mushroomed into a relational experience. It was like an image on a screen that came into focus, an image I had been looking at for a long time and had never thought could be any clearer. Even today as I try to write about it, words cannot capture what happened with those little sheep and shepherd as I sat on the floor hearing the familiar text of the parable. What I can say about that moment is that the journey changed. That lesson from the Catechesis of the Good Shepherd was not just a moment in time but has become an anchor in my life, a directional signpost along the journey, a map to untold wonders.

William Targett
Director,
Office of Formation for Discipleship
Catholic Pastoral Centre
Archdiocese of Toronto

Contents

Preface	1
Introduction	5
Chapter One: Telling the Stories	13
Part 1: Those Who Came Before	15
Part 2: Mapping the Experience	18
Part 3: The Experience: Steps on the Journey	22
Part 4: Introducing the Catechists	25
Chapter Two: Adults – Seven Companions	30
Part 1: The Call	31
Part 2: The Commitment	35
Part 3: The Challenge	39
Chapter Three:	
Children: A "Different Way of Being Christians"	47
Part 1: Spirituality of Childhood	48
Chapter Four: Being in Love	57
Part 1: Religious Experience	57
Part 2: Theology of Childhood	59
Part 3: The "Child as Parable"	61
Chapter Five: To The Sources	66
Part 1: Word of Life: Bible	66
Part 2: Food of Life: Liturgy	73
Chapter Six:	
Good News of Great Joy: the Christian Message	78
Part 1: Materials for the Message	78
Part 2: Meditation and Prayer	83

Chapter Seven: The Formative Presence of Children   91
    Part 1: Celebrating and Meditating with Children   91
    Part 2: The Atrium – Environment of Encounter   99
    Part 3: Gifts from Children   102

Chapter Eight: Dynamics of Relationship   110
    Part 1: Communion, Community, Mission   111
    Part 2: A Call within a Call   119
    Part 3: Learning Process:
    Information, Formation, Transformation   122

Chapter Nine: Ways of Accompaniment   128
    Part 1: Reflection   129
    Part 2: Observation   139

Chapter Ten: Journey Together   156
    Part 1: Images of Growth   157
    Part 2: Growing in Community   164

Epilogue: The Catechesis of the Good Shepherd – As a "Way"   171

Appendix A: Letter of Sofia Cavalletti (2009)   184

Appendix B: Letter of Sofia Cavalletti (2010)   186

Appendix C: Contemplation and Formation   191

Endnotes   203

Acknowledgments   216

About the Author   217

Photographs & Child's Drawing   218

Preface
Personally Speaking

Since this work is basically meant to be the story of others, I have tried to keep out of the way as far as possible and let them speak, especially the seven catechists whose experience it narrates. That said, those who kindly read this book in its various drafts advised that I say something on a personal level. So, I offer this brief background to indicate some of the main roots—remote and recent—out of which it grew, which I hope will be helpful.

A brief history: remote and recent

Allow me to begin with two events that happened a long time ago within the space of a month. In that month the first child of the next generation in our family was born and a beloved 9 year old girl died of leukemia. I was young and did not have the words to understand, much less express, the mystery of life and death these two beautiful children embodied. But, one decade later, I had found the words, after spending two years in Rome.

In 1975 I met Sofia Cavalletti—one of the major persons in these pages—first by letter, then in person during her first course on North American soil, in St. Paul, MN. A few months later I went to Rome to study with her and Gianna Gobbi, her closest colleague, and others associated with the children's center in Sofia's home. At that time it was still called by the name it was given, I suppose, when they began their work: the "Maria Montessori School of Religion."

Like Leaven

As it turned out, I was the first English-speaking, as well as Canadian, student to study with them in Rome. After two indescribable years, I returned home wanting to start in Toronto what I had seen and lived there. By "what" I mean their approach to the religious formation for children, and adults, which had no identifying name as yet. That was given by a Mexican bishop in the late 70s: the Catechesis of the Good Shepherd.

Back to the story. The year I returned home, Rev. Elliott Allen, Dean of the Faculty of Theology at the University of St. Michael's College, where I was completing my theology studies, invited Sofia to offer a three-week intersession course on their catechetical approach. Also, given the hearty response of the many people who attended it, he invited me to convert a seminar room in the Theology Faculty building, in which to prepare children from the adjacent parish who wanted to celebrate the sacraments of First Reconciliation and Eucharist.

Then in 1986, both Sofia and Gianna were invited by Bishop Aloysius Ambrozic, who would become Cardinal Archbishop of Toronto, and Bishop Marcel Gervais, who would become Archbishop of Ottawa, to come to Toronto to give a three-week international course for two consecutive summers. Now the interest in the catechesis was growing to the point where a systematic formation programme for adults was envisioned, to be co-sponsored by the Toronto Archdiocese and the University of St. Michael's College, affiliated with the University of Toronto.

With Sofia's and Gianna's help, once again, the three-cycle course for adults was proposed to the University of St. Michael's College. This proposal was accepted to be incorporated into their Continuing Education Division Certificate Programmes,

Preface

and it was proposed that I undertake further theological studies in service of establishing it.

The Doctor of Ministry Programme was most suitable for this purpose because a practical research project was part of its requirements. With the help of many wonderful people (hence the many names acknowledged at the end), we designed a pastoral research experience for catechists who were in the formation course and working with children at the same time.

Specifically, it was required to conduct this project using qualitative research, to write up the findings in an objective manner, to substantiate them with various resources, and finally to present it to a group of persons who had no knowledge of the catechesis. After the programme was completed, I sent the finished work to Sofia, then called: "A Way of Being with Children: Exploring the Catechesis of the Good Shepherd from a Pastoral Perspective." Sofia thought it would be helpful to those in the catechesis and agreed to write an introduction for it. Unfortunately, we never got back to it.

Jumping ahead another decade, a number of Sofia's and Gianna's books had been translated into English. Yet, there still seemed a need for something that focused specifically on the experience of catechists who companion children. Then came the invitation to make this document available—about which, more in the Introduction. In order to do that, a series of attempts have been made to render it in a more accessible form, as noted in the following points.

Format: By removing all the formal aspects relating to its academic requirements, e.g., qualitative research, it has been reduced substantially. For those who are aided by "visuals," some of the original charts, diagrams, etc. have been kept.

Like Leaven

Tone: As mentioned at the start, this work is intended to present the experience of others. This is why the objective tone has been retained, as have the pseudonyms used for the seven catechists in the original research project.

Detail: Since it is hoped that this will speak to those for whom this catechesis is a new world, the depth of detail has been kept. It is also hoped that the repetition this involves will not prove too tedious for those who are well-familiar with the catechesis.

Language: Also in consideration for those who are new to the catechesis, every attempt has been made to describe aspects and explain language common to it, and which otherwise could seem just jargon.

Endnotes: Many of the footnotes have been removed. Those that remain have been updated and revised, as is the case with the whole work, and moved to the end for those who may find footnotes unfriendly.

Photos: A few photos have been added from my first years in Rome, or sent to me by Sofia, at a time before digital technology. May that obvious failing be forgiven in favor of the personal face they offer.

Appendices: There seemed no better way to conclude this work than with two letters by Sofia Cavalletti, both written a year or two before her death (Appendix A and B). The third appendix contains the reflection that I wrote a few months after receiving the letter Sofia wrote in 2009, and her positive response to it encourages me to include it here.

It is hoped that these attempts will serve to make this work more reader-friendly, but there are surely many lacks. How consoling, then, are the words of Blessed Mother Teresa that we are not called to be successful; we are called to be faithful.

—Patricia Coulter

Introduction

The Catechesis of the Good Shepherd has been aptly described as an "approach to enabling children to live their religious potential."[1] It is important to add that this catechesis is also an approach to enabling adults to live their religious potential. Even though it has spread to over 37 countries on five continents, it is still being discovered, and thus many questions are asked about it.

Questions

One cluster of questions relates precisely to the experience of adults in this catechesis, and specifically about the preparation of catechists. Obviously many of these questions come from persons who are unfamiliar with the catechesis.

As an example, I draw on the unique experience of Tina Lillig. Since its beginning, Tina was the first Director of the first English-speaking National Association of the Catechesis of the Good Shepherd in the United States, right up until her death in 2009. For many years, Tina served in what was a sort of clearing house for the ever-expanding growth of the Catechesis. So, she was in a special position to hear such questions coming not only from people in the United States, Canada, and other English-speaking countries, but also from people in Mexico and other Spanish-speaking countries too.

Being at the hub of this community during the time of its emergence on North American soil, Tina's ear was always open not only to those representing its spokes within the catechesis, but also to those from various fields who are not familiar with it (henceforward referred to as CGS). Tina found that one of the most frequently asked questions concerned the preparation of adults who wished to serve as catechists. She noted:

> "People wonder: 'What kind of formation do these catechists have?' It's so very unique in any formation. Some others [programs for catechists] come close, but they do not receive the same life-commitment response that CGS does."

This book offers one response to this question about the preparation of catechists. It originates in an almost year-long research experience undertaken with a group of seven catechists focused on that very theme. Tina encouraged that the written account of that work be made available because:

> "There needs to be something that focuses on adult formation in the CGS: about the principles, about the adult's encounter with scripture and liturgy, about the materials. And it has to be someone who has done this formation."

We hope this book will be helpful for those who wish to know something—or perhaps something more—about the catechesis from this perspective. We are thinking particularly of pastors and parents, teachers and catechists, and all those wishing to nourish the religious lives of children.

In responding to questions about the adult learning process in this catechesis, we touch on the foundations that are helpful for nurturing the child's religious potential in the context of home, parish, and school. More particularly, we will explore some key elements usually found in any form of catechist preparation, such as Bible and liturgy, with an emphasis on how these scriptural and liturgical themes are approached in this catechesis.

Introduction

More Questions

There is another cluster of questions about the experience of adults in this catechesis. These come from persons who are familiar with the catechesis, or who are actually involved in it, or who have already completed the catechist preparation in the CGS. For instance, this excerpt is from a letter written by someone who has completed all three courses for catechists, and is now involved in guiding other adults in their learning process:

> "Why is there such an emphasis on theology when we're preparing to work with young children? Why is the formation so long? How do we nourish our spiritual life? How do we trust the Holy Spirit to "do the work"? How do we let go of our own sense of "omnipotence" (my own favorite temptation)? How is the atrium an aid for the catechist? What is it about the CGS that fosters such a sense of community?"

First, we will address these more detailed questions on the level of the theological and educational principles that undergird the catechist preparation process. Then we will focus on some pastoral aspects that are important in this approach with respect to the preparation of catechists. We will do this in a very concrete way, namely, through the personal accounts—written and verbal—of seven catechists who share about their experience narrated here. This experience includes both their catechist course as well as their ministry with children.

Overview

Since this work grew out of the experience of these catechists, we wanted it to reflect the organic unfolding of their experience.

Thus it is written primarily in the form of a narrative, in keeping with their stories, which flow through the entire work. Also, the text is interspersed with various charts, diagrams, etc., which hopefully will help to illustrate the narrative in a synthetic form.

For those who may be new to this catechesis, the first chapter begins by describing some of its basic elements. Then the story begins immediately in a personalized way. We situate the research journey in its living context, with real-life people. That is, this chapter introduces the catechists, maps their experience, and looks at the settings in which their course and ministry with children took place.

This early entry into the experience of these seven catechists is due to the fact that this catechesis is still relatively unknown, as we said. For example, when asked about this ministry it is common to hear: "What's that?" Or when showing someone the prepared environment (called *atrium*) to be asked: "What are those toys? Where can I buy them?"

Chapter Two opens the door into some of the themes of their experience. It begins with three themes that emerged at the outset: 1) the call, 2) commitment, and 3) challenge the CGS represents for these catechists. These themes are described from their own perspective.

This provides a concrete backdrop against which to highlight some of the features of the religious world of children in Chapter Three. Here we address the spirituality of children that undergirds this catechesis.

Chapter Four continues this exploration into the religious experience of children and presents some important theological aspects of childhood. Following this is a synopsis of Cavalletti's

Introduction

scriptural vision of the child, based on her profound biblical scholarship and her lengthy experience with children. Sofia delves into the words of Jesus in the Gospels, and offers valuable insights into the child as a living "parable".

This gives a solid base upon which to build the accounts of the catechists' experience in Chapter Five. They begin with the essential sources of nourishment and means of empowerment for these catechists: scripture and liturgy.

In Chapter Six, two other elements in their preparation process are detailed: 1) the biblical-liturgical materials especially designed for children; 2) and the way they are presented to children, both of which are seen as formative for adults as well. Then Chapter Seven looks at how the children themselves can be a formative presence for adults. Some of the contributions children offer these catechists are singled out.

Chapter Eight focuses on the heart of the catechists' journey: the dynamic of relationship. This dynamic is looked at in terms of three movements that were discerned in the catechists' accounts: 1) the first relates to communion, community and mission; 2) the second to conversion; 3) and the third to the many levels discovered within the course and ministry experiences.

Chapter Nine focuses on the catechists' exercise of two activities: reflection and observation. While basic to this catechesis, these activities were given special emphasis in this small group experience as exercises to develop the spiritual faculty of attentiveness. Thus these two activities are examined in detail through the catechists' first-person accounts. As well, mention is made of some of the pastoral implications their accounts contain.

Chapter Ten presents a retrospective of our time together, from a distance of many months. This chapter has two parts, which includes signposts in terms of what may be helpful in the future preparation of catechists. The first part looks at the catechists' images for their experience, which point to the transformative potential within this catechesis. The second part attends to the significance and role of community in ministry, also expressed in the catechists' own words.

The Epilogue presents a perspective revealed in the catechists' summary of their experience, which emerged only with the passage of time. That is, from what these catechists shared at the end of their small group journey, the image of this catechesis as a "way" appeared, a preview of which is offered below in chart form.

Finally, we conclude with two letters of Sofia Cavalletti as a postscript to this work (contained in the appendices). They were written when she was in her 90s and embody the spirit of this catechesis in a special way. The first is Sofia's 2009 letter, in which she literally sings with joy about the news she received during a visit of Sisters from the Missionaries of Charity community (Appendix A). The second is Sofia's 2010 letter, in which she looks back across her life in the catechesis—her "marvelous adventure" (Appendix B).

The last appendix contains my reflection on Sofia's 2009 letter. Although it was written for those engaged in this catechesis, as was this letter of Sofia's, we hope that it might speak to those who may be new to this catechesis as well.

Introduction

The Good Shepherd Catechesis: as a "Way"

Eileen
- A different way of looking at children.
- Being, just remaining and we are with the children in this way.

Francesca
- Different rhythms and stages…because everything changes.
- I got a gift…this prayer that I was able to do.

Kate
- Being in this way is good.
- That's what we're doing with the children—letting the light shine in.

Ruth
- The way you present things.
- The way you speak with the children.
- The way you respect each moment.
- The way you let the moment happen.

Mary
- Anyone can try to show this way to others.
- Another way to find God.
- The natural way.
- A beautiful way.

Like Leaven

Domenica
- The Spirit flowing…to the children and from the child in me.
- Peace and joy.
- It's a kind of cycle. You touch me, I touch you, and we're touching God together.

Wendy
- First the catechesis was like falling in love; now I'm settling down inside.
- It's something we do with our hands, with all of our senses.
- A different way of relating to children.

Chapter One:
Telling the Stories

To indicate the general orientation of this work as a whole, a symbol is taken from *The Hidden Mountain*, Gabrielle Roy's portrayal of a French Canadian artist, Pierre Cadorai. Pierre travels the mostly untravelled northern reaches of Canada in search of perfecting his craft. Pierre's unrealizable dream of seeing the works of the European masters unexpectedly becomes possible, and so he sets out on his first trip to Paris.

An important moment in this man's solitary sojourn occurs at one point during his Atlantic crossing. Standing by the rail of the ship's deck, stooped over and wrapt by the movement of wind and water, we hear Pierre's musings on a phrase from Shakespeare: "[Pierre] lifted his head, repeated to himself: "To tell my story… Yes, such was the deep desire of every life, the longing of every soul…"[2]

That phrase, "to tell the story", captures the intent as well as the form of the following work. It is a telling of stories, on various levels. Principally, the narrative is woven around the stories of seven catechists. At another level are the stories of Sofia Cavalletti and Gianna Gobbi, initiators of this catechesis, as well of Dr. Maria Montessori, whose educational principles they developed in this catechesis.

It is important to say at the outset that this is a very limited work. In presenting the stories of these seven catechists, this work does not purport to do more than explore one small area of the catechesis. In this sense, it is a study in miniature, like one of Pierre's paintings of his "resplendent" mountain in Labrador, depicted in a space that "was not twice the size of a man's hand."[3] This work is also similar to a work in miniature in that there is a density of detail, but it is one in which, like Cadorai's sketch, opened "what might be called a perspective"[4] on this catechesis.

That shipboard moment in Pierre's crossing to a new world, also offers a symbol both of how this experience configured itself and how it will unfold here. Even at its inception, this journey presented itself in terms of setting forth toward new territory, represented by the experience of the seven catechists in formation for ministry with children. As will be seen, the journey metaphor appears as a recurring symbol in the catechists' accounts. As well, that shipboard scene throws light on an inner dynamic underlying this small group experience. In all its phases, the research process was similar to that moment when

> Pierre held himself stooping forward, like a tree listening to itself sing. "To tell my story…" The human being cast forth upon the waters its humble, its modest, its so legitimate request.[5]

There is one difference, however. In this case it is listening to the stories of others, and this is not an easy task because, to quote the words of Kate, one of the catechists in this work, "often there's a struggle before you get to that story at the end." Right from the beginning there will be constant references to these seven catechists, who will be speaking in their own words, since this work attempts to give voice to their interior experience as they grow in relationship with God, each other, the children and the catechesis.

Chapter One: Telling Stories

Part I: Those Who Came Before

The Good Shepherd Catechesis addresses the religious capacities and needs of children approximately between the ages of 3-12 years. It began in 1954 at the Center of Catechesis in Rome established by Sofia Cavalletti (+2011) and Gianna Gobbi (+2002). Since then it has rooted itself in very diverse social settings, as well as in different Christian churches. The pedagogical principles of this catechesis are informed by Dr. Maria Montessori's vision of education in general and religious education in particular.

Dr. Maria Montessori (1870-1952), one of Italy's first women medical doctors, moved from the field of medicine into education. The aim of her psycho-pedagogical method was to educate the human potential of children. Montessori's innovative work also included a brief foray into the area of religious education. The first children's *atrium* was founded in 1915 in Barcelona, Spain, according to her guidelines. More will be said later about specific educational principles in Montessori's work that are significant in the practice of this catechesis. For now it is enough to let Montessori tell her story of a defining moment in her life which appears to her as full of "mystery" and "wonder":

> "What happened more than thirty years ago now, will always remain mystery to me. I have tried since then to understand what took place in those children. Certainly there was nothing of what is to be found now in any House of Children. There were only large rough tables… What was the wonder due to? No one could state it clearly. But it conquered me forever, because it penetrated my heart as a new light. One day I looked at them with eyes which saw them differently and I asked

myself, "Who are you, are you the same children you were before?" And I said within myself: "Perhaps you are those children of whom it was said that they would come to save humanity. If so, I shall follow you". Since then, I am she who tries to grasp their message and to follow them. And in order to follow them, I changed my whole life. I was nearly 40. I had in front of me a doctor's career and a professorship at the University. But I left all, because I felt compelled to follow them, and to find others who could follow them, for I saw that in them lay the secret of the soul."[6]

Sofia and Gianna, as we said, initiated this catechesis. Sofia, who had never met Montessori personally, brought her years of biblical scholarship to this work. Gianna, who knew and collaborated in a course with Montessori, brought her years of experience in Montessori centers for young children. Together they dedicated themselves to educating the religious potential of children. In doing so they began to build on Montessori's pedagogical principles and insights in the religious sphere, as well as the contributions of others who undertook religious education initiatives deriving from Montessori's work.[7] Three basic aspects of this catechesis are outlined in chart form at the end of the chapter.

In the year before her death, Sofia summarized the story of the beginnings of their catechesis in a letter she wrote in acceptance of the Catherine of Siena Award from Aquinas Institute of Theology in St. Louis, Missouri (see Appendix B). She describes the "marvelous adventure" that began for her and Gianna in 1954 with just a few children:

> With that first group of children in 1954, we had decided to read together the first account of creation

Chapter One: Telling Stories

in Genesis, a reading that took almost two hours, so that it was then time to go home. But—and this is the beginning of the adventure for us adults—Paolo was there in the group. Paolo was six or seven years old. He had resisted coming that day because it meant giving up the one afternoon he had free during the week. Yet, when the moment came to end the session and go home and not come back for a whole week, his big, black eyes filled with tears."

When Paolo's eyes filled with tears, because he did not want the session to end, it became a defining moment for Sofia and Gianna:

We can say that Paolo showed us the direction of our lives. Later we began to hear stories of similar responses of the children at the end of the 2-hour atrium session when it was time to go home, and these responses were coming from atria in an ever–increasing variety of socio-economic settings. Thus we began to wonder, "Who are the children?" What kind of relationship does God have with the human creature in the earliest stage of life?

I conclude this section by offering what was to become a defining moment for me in this catechesis. During the second year of my study in Rome, I spent time with Maria, a child under the age of three who was staying in a children's hospital in Rome. For brevity's sake, here is Sofia's distillation of that experience:

"There is a story of little Maria—she was 2½ years and very sick with cancer in a hospital in Rome. She was very lonely, very sick. It was impossible to establish a relationship with her. I tried everything I could but didn't even get a glance from her. The other children said she scarcely spoke and often wept quite alone (the family lived far to the south so she was alone in the hospital). A co-worker of mine went and presented the [Good Shepherd] parable. At first Maria seemed to be asleep or at least very far away, but when it was finished and the materials were being gathered up the child suddenly jumped on the bed and showed quite clearly that she wanted to listen once again to the parable. The catechist presented it again and the child jumped into her lap, kissed her and wanted to be fed by her, when dinner arrived. The night nurse knew nothing of this, but later said that Maria had started singing and saying: "He knows my name." This fact had struck her."[8]

Part 2: Mapping the Experience:
Formation Course and Ministry with Children

Two dimensions of the small group research experience are related here. One is the catechists' participation in a formation course. The second is their involvement in ministry with children. Before delving into their actual experience, it is important to detail some of the components of the landscape of these two worlds.

A) **Formation Course:** the course that these seven catechists were involved in has some distinguishing qualities, like all formation courses in this catechesis. Here are three:

1) There is a vital interconnection between content and method in the catechesis with children. Sofia clarifies it this way:

   In our estimation, the choice of method is

Chapter One: Telling Stories

related to the question of content. There are certain contents that cannot be communicated except by certain methodologies. The method is not like an empty box that can be filled with anything whatsoever; the method has a soul, and this soul should correlate to the content that is being transmitted through the method. Between method and content there should be a profound accord, an affinity of nature; otherwise there is the risk of distorting the content.[9]

This interconnection is reflected in the adult formation programme. That is, the integration of the thematic content with the practice with children.

Therefore, this small group experience highlighted elements explicitly designed to encourage this integration. The first is the catechist's written observations of children. The second is the catechists' written reflections: one focused on the course, the other on the children, and both detailed at the end of this chapter.

2) The methodology of the adult course reflects the Montessori orientation; for example, the use of certain materials and the prepared environment for children (*atrium*). Also, the three levels addressed in the catechesis for children are mirrored in the three-tiered structure for the adult course. That is, there is an essential coherence between the child's developmental stages in terms of the structure and content of the adult course: first level, for children 3-6 years; second level, for children 6-9 years; third level, for children 9-12 years approximately.

3) Finally, the content of the adult course has three basic

components which correspond to the three foci in the catechesis with children.

a) **the biblical and liturgical foundation:** especially relating to the biblical and liturgical themes presented to children.

b) **the pedagogical dimension:** particularly the psycho-pedagogical principles underlying Dr. Montessori's educational work.

c) **the methodological dimension:** relative to the biblical-liturgical materials, which are designed to help the children's meditation and prayer.

A practical application of this last point (c) is that catechists prepare their own handbook, called *album*, for all the materials associated with a particular course level. The *album* addresses various aspects, such as: the biblical and liturgical sources; the point of the Christian message to be proclaimed to the children; how to present each theme with its specific material to the children, and so forth.

As we said, we highlight these elements because they are operative in the course as experienced by these seven catechists. In their case, they participated in the second level course, namely, to prepare them for ministry with children aged 6-9. For the purpose of this small research group, we focused only on one segment of the second level course; this is the context of their course experience narrated here.

B) **Ministry with Children:** As we also mentioned, all these catechists were serving in a parish atrium with children of this age group. So, it was essential that this experience also be included. Practically speaking, this amounts to a layered experience. It encompasses two intrinsically linked components in the catechists' experience: their formation course and their atrium experience. This atrium component contributed to an inclusive approach and it allowed for an exploration of the whole formation process of each person.

The Focus

The main thrust of this research experiment with these seven catechists was to explore if, and in what way, this catechesis might serve as a means of helping adults to accompany children on their spiritual journey in a *mutually formative* manner. That is, does the formation course not only prepare adults to nurture children, but also to be nurtured by them?

Yes, the focus of the catechist formation course is directed to helping children be "not only in touch but in communion, in intimacy, with Jesus Christ"—in keeping with the "definitive aim of catechesis."[10] Yet, how and in what way does it also attend to the spirituality of the adult as well? Put another way, we are addressing how to nourish the adult's own spirituality, as Sofia highlights here:

> The first point I think necessary to clarify is that, if a spiritual characteristic of the *catechist* of the Good Shepherd exists, the characteristic must be an expression of the soul of our work; if such a spirituality has to take some shape, this shape must emerge from inside our work and must adhere very closely to it. The path is already indicated by the principal aim of our association: "To involve adults and children in a common religious experience, in which the religious values of childhood are predominant... And then the problem arises of how to nourish it."[11] (emphasis mine)

Why is this an important question in researching this small group of catechists? Because they were not just an ad hoc group brought together temporarily for the purpose of experimenting with the formation course. In fact, they had already completed the first level course, and they all had been involved in the atrium with children for at least three years. Thus, to focus on exploring what sustains these catechists in their long-haul commitment in this ministry is central to this experience.

Part 3: The Experience:
Steps on the Journey

Before introducing the seven catechists, it is helpful to give a basic outline of their journey together as a small group. The following is a brief overview of its phases and features.

A) Phases:

1) Our time together began with a **preparatory period**, in which the catechists were invited to discuss the purpose of this small group experience. During this period the catechists were given certain information about the process, as well as a series of initial questions to reflect upon.

2) This was followed by a **three month phase** (from April to June). It was composed of two components we mentioned: A) the formation course and B) the atrium experience. Both of these occurred at approximately the same time. The biblical and liturgical themes presented during this 3-month segment of the course are outlined at the end of this chapter.

Chapter One: Telling Stories

a) For 15 minutes at the end of the **course session**, each catechist was invited to engage in a simple reflective journal exercise, in response to the following questions:

- "What topic/theme was presented in this session?
- In what way was I touched by it? And why?"

b) During this same 3-month period, the catechists' **atrium involvement** included: the time of preparing children for the sacraments of First Eucharist and Reconciliation, as well as the retreat dedicated to the celebration of these sacraments.

Each catechist was invited to 1) observe the children, and 2) reflect upon their experience with the children, especially by means of the following two journal exercises:

Children's Session: Observations	Date
In attending to the children, what did you notice…see…hear…and so forth?	

Children's Session: Reflections	Date
Take ten minutes to make a note to yourself of what this time with the children has said to you.	

3) After the summer break, the group gathered together in the fall for a **first reflection day**. All were invited to reflect on their experience of the course and with the children. Our facilitator for this communal moment was Brother Ignatius Feaver, a spiritual director who has a long friendship with Sofia and association with the catechesis.

4) We met again for a **final reflection day** the following January. This communal gathering allowed us the opportunity to look back many months later on the experience as a whole. Once again, Brother Ignatius guided our reflection time together.

a) **Some Features:**

The responses of the seven catechists recorded here are taken from all the phases outlined above. Most of their responses were in written form. Some were in oral form, and then transcribed verbatim later. Thus, throughout this work each of these catechists will be speaking in her own words.

There was a cumulative effect of repeatedly reading, listening to, and reflecting on their responses throughout the chronological sequence of our journey. What started out simply as impressions and associations gradually began to coalesce coherently. The effect was akin to moving through a terrain whose originally indecipherable features slowly become clear. The following are some overall features that seemed to characterize their experience:

- They describe a rich—cognitively and affectively—and multi-layered world (including dimensions of interiority as well as exteriority).
- It is above all a relational world, composed of seven interconnected spheres.
- The axis of this relational dynamic is their relationship with God.
- There is a pervasive presence of children (even in their accounts of the course, when children

are absent) that is identifiable as formative for them.

Finally, the interconnected spheres mentioned above include the relationship with:

- God – oneself – children – the catechists in the course – the catechists in this small group – the formation course – the Good Shepherd catechesis as a whole.

Part 4: Introducing the Catechists

"Catechesis is at the heart of the Church's mission."[12]

A significant aspect of this group of seven is that it represents a sampling of catechists active in this ministry from 4 to 11 years, as we said; as such they provide valuable insights into the world of this catechesis. The end of this section contains brief biographical sketches of each of the catechists' personal, professional and pastoral background. Some of the general and specific commonalities relating to this catechist group are schematized below.

Generally, the Catechists are:

- laywomen in their 30s and 40s (this preponderance of women is representative of, but not exclusive to, the Good Shepherd catechesis);
- in the Roman Catholic tradition (except one, who comes from the Anglican tradition);
- married (presently or previously);
- mothers (except one) who are professionally trained, and serving as volunteer catechists (except one).

Specifically, the Catechists are:

- in the course (as a Certificate Programme, Continuing Education Division, University of St. Michael's College,), and involved in a (2-3 day) sacramental retreat with children (in their parish-based atrium);
- participating in the atrium in different capacities. Some have more responsibility for facilitating the children's group, and others are assisting them;
- some are participating in the retreat for the first time. Others have many years' experience in preparing children for the reception of the sacraments of First Eucharist and Reconciliation.

Catechesis of the Good Shepherd: Three Characteristics

1) It is experimental in nature. This is a key feature in the 32 points of reflection on "The Spirit of the Catechesis": "The Catechesis of the Good Shepherd has an experimental character and is open to go always deeper into the infinite mystery of God and God's cosmic covenant with God's creatures."[13] For example, Sofia and Gianna worked uninterruptedly with children for over five decades.

2) It continues to be tested as to its validity in service to children, with the support of a network of collaborators, which is international in scope. The collaborative spirit is a hallmark of the CGS, as instanced in the early-formed association, the "Maria Montessori Association for the Religious Formation of the Child," begun in Rome in 1963. In 1996 a more formal and broadly international Council (*Consiglio*, in Italian) was formed with representatives from all the countries where the CGS is rooted.

Chapter One: Telling Stories

3) As indicated above, this catechesis employs a dynamic rather than a static approach. As a result, it is evolving in terms of its content and methodology for children and adults. This involves a constant commitment to researching and refining its content and methodology in terms of its adequacy to nurture children's religious potential.

An important point linked to this is the insistence by Sofia and Gianna that the curriculum be in service of the children, as they note in their "Curriculum Outline for Children":

> "The outline is intended only as an orientation or indication to help you arrange your calendar with children. It developed from and is based on the religious capacities of the child. Therefore the *actual curriculum*—the sequence and timing of presenting the various themes of the Christian message—*depends on the individual child and the nature of the group of children.*"[14] (authors' emphasis)

The Seven Catechists: Biographical Sketch

Eileen: mother of four children, is an early childhood educator, with a specialization in developmentally challenged children. She has been involved in an atrium for 11 years and is the only catechist in this group who is a facilitator in the first level adult course (to serve children 3-6 years of age).

Francesca: mother of two children, had been a home economist, food and consumer consultant, and writer. She first began her CGS involvement as a parent when her two children came to the atrium. Then she founded an atrium in her parish, and is its full-time director, and part of the parish staff.

Kate: mother of four children, is a chartered accountant, working on a self-employed, part-time basis. Previously a lay pastoral associate for three years, she has been involved in the catechesis for nine years, serving as the co-founder and director of her parish atrium.

Ruth: mother of two adopted children, is a full-time nurse, with a specialization in lung cancer clinical research. She began her involvement with this catechesis as a parent. Since taking the first level course, she has worked in her parish atrium, including three First Eucharist and Reconciliation retreats for children.

Domenica: mother of three children, is presently teaching in a Catholic high school. Her interest in the CGS began as a parent as well. Since beginning her formation, she has been observing as well as assisting in the atrium. This is her first time participating in the children's retreat.

Mary: mother of two children, is an elementary school teacher. She also began her association with this catechesis as a parent, and since her first course she has participated as part of a catechist team. This is also her first time participating in the children's retreat.

Wendy: is a business educator in human resources and administration. She has been involved in a parish atrium for three years. This is her first time participating in a special retreat to prepare the children for, and celebrate the sacrament of, First Reconciliation.

Chapter One: Telling Stories

Formation Course: Themes and Resources

Themes

The True Vine parable (John 15): biblical background and presentation.

The evangelical maxims of Jesus; about moral formation.

The rite of the sacrament of Reconciliation: background and celebration with children

The rite of the Eucharist (Eucharistic Prayer IV): background.

First Eucharist and Reconciliation: in the context of children's sacramental retreat.

Background on and presentation of: "The Mystery of Faith"; the "Synthesis of the Mass"; the "Gestures of Gift" in the Eucharist (epiclesis, offering, the breaking of the bread, and the exchange of peace).

Background on and presentation of the first "History of the Kingdom of God" Timeline: The Unity of the Kingdom.

Resources

See the following works by Sofia Cavalletti for detailed information about these themes:

The History of the Kingdom of God, Part 2: Liturgy and the Building of the Kingdom

The Religious Potential of the Child 6 to 12 Years Old

Ways to Nurture the Relationship with God

See the endnotes for specific citations in relation to various themes mentioned by the catechists.

Chapter Two:
Adults: Seven Companions

This chapter enters into the experience of these seven catechists. Three themes began to emerge from their written accounts, even before we came together as a small group for the first time.

The first is the theme of vocation. Call is the foundation on which their experience builds. It is implicit in the first set of their personal statements. The second theme is their commitment to a specific call, represented by their involvement in the CGS. To understand more about the nature of their commitment, we single out a few elements particular to the CGS that undergird their personal statements (part two).

The third theme is the challenge. It begins to be heard from our inaugural meeting as a group, when we discussed the nature, purpose and instruments of our time together —such as the reflection and observation activities we mentioned. The catechists' responses revealed not only the specific aspect of challenge inherent in taking the journey together as a small group, but also in this catechesis in general. We explore this theme by presenting their personal responses as expressed at this initial meeting (part three).

Chapter Two: Adults: Two Companions

Part 1: The Call

Prior to our first gathering as a group, each catechist was invited to write their response to this question: "What brought you to the Catechesis of the Good Shepherd? The thematic of vocation emerges clearly in their catechists' written responses.

Before presenting the catechists words, we note six characteristics with respect to the general and specific vocation of these laywomen. In some cases these characteristics will be presented in dialogue with various Church documents, so as to lift up the ecclesial nature of their call.

1) Each catechist is actively pursuing her primary vocation as a Christian layperson.

    This embraces the individual's involvement in ministry/apostolate, namely, spreading the Gospel, especially to children.

2) In all but one case, this is lived also with their own children, in the context of the value they ascribe to the family as the "domestic Church" (Dogmatic Constitution on the Church, 11). And they are exercising the "very important creativity" involved in the commitment to the "spiritual dimension" of motherhood" (*The Dignity and Vocation of Women*, 19-20).

3) All are catechists on behalf of the larger ecclesial community. So, it can be said that each has responded to a specific call: "At the origin of the catechist's vocation, therefore, apart from the sacraments of baptism and confirmation, there is a specific call from the Holy Spirit, a *"special charism recognized by the Church"*[15] (document's emphasis).

Personal Statements

Eileen   "I had finished my work at the Developmental Centre (due to pregnancy)…we had been meeting as a group in order to set up a new atrium. The formation drew me in and benefitted me personally. I decided to go and receive the formal training. Since then it has been vital for the catechesis to be a very large part of my life and the life of my family. It has always been a way to truly live my (our) faith."

Francesca   "I was called! A desire to find out how to serve children in the Roman Catholic church. I was a convert, in charge of a Sunday morning liturgy program, with no direction or materials from the Catholic Church. When I heard that someone would be speaking about children and the Catholic Church, I attended an evening [seminar about catechesis]. I soon fell in love with what [was] said and wanted my 2 children to take part in an atrium experience. Soon after that, I realized that I wanted to hear more and more…just for me. I was hooked. I felt I had arrived home. The children in the atrium have helped keep me in the catechesis."

Chapter Two: Adults: Two Companions

Kate "1) the fact that the child is at the centre of this work; the love and respect for the child and his/her needs is clearly central;

2) This desire is particularly strong because the nature of the work is dynamic and changing/improving based on the needs of the child and…partly met by my own research and partly through other courses…

3) making materials has offered me a wonderful opportunity to work with my hands…[and] has kept me connected to the very essentials;

4) the *integrity* of the work…a deep understanding of our faith, of the Bible and liturgy."

Ruth "Interest in assisting as my child was involved."

Mary "I was waiting with another mother from [parish] while our children took ballet. I was new to the parish and heard for the first time [about] the miniature world in the choir loft… [Another mother was] telling me she did not worry about the spirituality of her children because they were participating in the atrium. How could anyone have such assurance about a class? (I wanted to know more.)

The next September my two children began in the atrium."

Domenica "A friend suggested the programme for my then two-and-a-half-year-old daughter A. Curiosity and interest on how to follow up on what my children revealed to me about their experiences at the atrium… The atmosphere in the atrium, the quiet in there… I really wanted to know more… how to achieve the peace, the joy and the love the children experienced in the atrium… I wanted to experience over and over again that same joy and awe in Our Lord."

Wendy "I have been a liturgical minister for approximately eight years. The parish priest at the time asked me if I would be willing to give 'private' catechism lessons to three children… who appeared to be having difficulty in the classroom setting… During this time I realized how much I enjoyed working with children… It has been the combination of my interest in education and children that has brought me to the catechesis."

In reading their excerpts, three more characteristics contained in this call can be detected:

4) Each catechist has a particular "interest" in, or has been "drawn" to, the CGS. As Francesca puts it: "The children in the atrium have helped keep me in the catechesis. They energize me." In these excerpts it is apparent that children assume an important role for them. Thus they indicate the contribution children make in the Church:

Chapter Two: Adults: Two Companions

> "It must be acknowledged that valuable possibilities exist even in the life's stages of infancy and childhood, both for the building up of the Church and for making society more humane"(*Vocation and Mission of the Lay Faithful*, no. 47).

5) This contribution of children is also seen as the reason for "wanting to help others receive these wonderful gifts" (Domenica), thus illustrating why

> "Jesus exalted the active role that little ones have in the Kingdom of God. They are the eloquent symbol and exalted image of those moral and spiritual conditions that are essential for entering into the Kingdom of God and for living the logic of total confidence in the Lord" (*Vocation and Mission of the Lay Faithful*, no. 47).

6) Finally, these excerpts suggest that this small group is, as is the CGS community in general, a microcosm of an larger ecclesial community, in which there is " a diversity and a complementarity," and in which each person "offers a totally unique contribution" (*Vocation and Mission of the Lay Faithful*, no. 20).

Part 2: The Commitment

Commitment is a melodic strain heard throughout our entire time together. It begins here at its start, audible already in these excerpts, and in other more explicit expressions from their personal statements. For example:

> "What has drawn me to, and kept me in the work over the past nine years" (Kate).

> "Help[ing] with a group of 3-6 year olds really cemented my commitment" (Domenica).

It is also the note on which our final day of reflection together concludes:

> "We're the ones who got really involved and committed" (Francesca).

> "It's about…staying by your commitment and fulfilling your need and the children's need" (Domenica).

This commitment has some specific aspects specific to this catechesis, which are already identifiable in the above excerpts, especially Kate's. They are:

- the environment of the atrium;
- the materials;
- the service of the catechist in relation to these two elements, but above all in relation to the child.

More will be said later about these three aspects. Only a brief word about each will be said here for two reasons. First, to clarify the nature of these catechists' commitment. Second, to offer necessary background for those who may be new to this catechesis.

A) The Atrium

As we have said, all the catechists are engaged in catechesis with children ages 6-9 in the atrium setting. The atrium, as Gianna Gobbi describes it in her important work, *Listening to God with Children*, is a prepared environment which

> "corresponds to the vital religious needs of the child, a

place where the child can experience religious life and can come to know the realities which feed this life."[16]

The atrium may be seen as a spiritual retreat centre. For example: Gianna writes that the atrium "has a special atmosphere which helps children to listen to the Christian message... This room or space is an environment where the child's activity unfolds in a meditative and prayerful manner."[17] The preparation of and care for this atrium environment is part of the commitment of these catechists.

B) The Materials

The atrium is furnished with specially designed materials for the children based on various biblical and liturgical themes. These materials, as indicated above, are not meant as a "teaching aid" for the adult, but rather to help the child's meditation and prayer. As such, the catechist's commitment in this catechesis involves not only learning about the biblical and liturgical themes offered to children. It also involves learning about the way these sources are introduced to children by means of these materials. This implies a sound preparation on the part of the catechist, as well as a significant commitment both in terms of time and practice. In addition, the catechist is encouraged to make as many of these materials as possible (further noted in Chapter 7).

C) The Catechist

Gianna Gobbi's book, *Listening to God with Children*, offers an in-depth treatment of the adult's role in this catechesis. There are also the many references to the catechist in Sofia's writings. For example, Sofia provides a succinct synthesis on this subject in her final work, *Way of Holy Joy*.[18] Suffice it to say now that a primary role of the catechist is to initiate the children into the Christian message, including the way it is "materialized" in the concrete biblical and liturgical materials.

To return to our seven catechists, they are practised in presenting the foundational themes of the Christian message to the youngest children (under six years). Since their present course and atrium experiences relate to children 6-8/9 years, the following excerpt is offered. It both highlights these catechists' commitment, as well as amplifies some of the themes they are studying:

- For children between ages six and nine, the new parabolic image of God is the True Vine, a Trinitarian representation of God, where the disciple's role is not just to stay close and follow (as with the Good Shepherd), but actually to participate in the life of the Vine.

- A timeline of the history of the kingdom of God highlights the three great moments in salvation history: creation, redemption and parousia, while inviting the children to ponder what they are being called to write on the "blank page" of history that is being lived now.

- We visualize the Bible as a library of books, using a box filled with small wooden models, colour coded for Old and New Testament, to represent each book of the Bible.

- As preparation for first Reconciliation, the children are first assured of the mercy of God through the parables of the Lost Sheep, the Lost Coin, and the Forgiving Father. Only then are they introduced to the Great Commandment and a work called "The Maxims," which highlights specific moral directives of Jesus and helps the children to examine their conscience. Mass-centered presentations continue to foster not only an understanding of, but also a great

Chapter Two: Adults: Two Companions

hunger for, the Eucharist.[19]

Certainly these three aspects—the atrium, the materials, the service of the catechist—represent a substantial commitment on the part of these catechists. As a result, certain challenges may arise. Within this framework, we now address some of the challenges inherent in the CGS in general, and this research process in particular.

Part 3: The Challenge

When we met for the first time as a small group, the catechists voiced their expectations, interpretations and attitudes in relation to the overall process we were beginning to undertake together. We also discussed the nature and purpose of what we would be doing, such as the basic instruments to aid their reflection and observation we mentioned earlier.

The catechists entered into the group experience in various ways. Some are enthusiastic: Francesca is ready to "just write and put in all kinds of things." Others seem ambivalent. Wendy candidly admits, "I feel protective of it [CGS] at this point…if I sound a little sensitive, it's because it means so much for me to be here." All are eager to help each other probe questions and aspects of interest. And challenges appeared, on two levels.

On one level, there were specific challenges posed by this small group journey. These were indicated in this first meeting, from which the following verbatim accounts are taken. On another level, these following excerpts suggest challenges which relate to the larger framework of the CGS itself. With respect to this level of challenge, some additional references will be made to persons both within and outside the CGS ministry.

Eileen:
"Why are we like that?"

"The mystery though, that we're trying to penetrate [is] we have people who have been in this work, and in it like [we] are. We don't come and go. So why are we like that? Let's penetrate that mystery...We know we want to be there...but somebody looking at this goes, 'Why?'...Everybody's benefitting...there's a ministry to adults happening at exactly the same time [as with children]. I think it's also helpful for us to even look at that...to start to go 'Why?'"

In this meeting, as at other times for Eileen, the catechist's personal formation is her focus: "Look at the catechesis and the hours and preparation. But we don't think of it that way, because we think of it as our formation." There is an important question at the base of "the mystery": "Why?" Others have voiced questions like hers, namely about what makes one commit to what has been described as "a long novitiate"[20] and singled out as demanding:

> "...catechists...occupy a far less than dictatorial role... [and] must completely trust the power of [the] message..."[21]

What is noteworthy is this catechist's openness to "penetrate" what is mysterious, even to herself.

Francesca:
"How to let go and trust?"

"I [have] some really crucial questions to address as a person, as a woman... When you actually take this catechesis and walk through it in moments in your life,

Chapter Two: Adults: Two Companions

through your ups and your downs and your crises, it's like a true test of just where you are. It's so affirming and it's so wonderful to have that…and I want to open everything up…I'm thinking, it's this catechesis! It gives you life, but it kills you…! I think it's basically: how do we take what we're doing with the children and live it in our own lives? Really learning to let go and to trust, and walk in a way that meets our needs as individuals, and to be as we were created to be? It's to balance; there's incredible highs, and there's lows, but it's this whole picture together."

Francesca is the only catechist in our small group who is employed full-time in the catechesis. As such, the challenges of this commitment are keenly felt by her. Elsewhere in her personal statement, Francesca asserts this catechesis to be "more demanding and challenging than any other thing I do," hence her need for trust in continuing in this commitment. With characteristic candour she asserts: "I don't want to minimize my life by covering up the struggle." Nor does she want her story "whitewashed." This is an important reminder for those of us involved in adult faith formation and catechesis:

> "Above all, one must begin by *accepting adults where they are…* It is essential to keep in mind the specific adults with whom one is working, their cultural background, human and religious needs, their expectations, faith experiences, and their potential. It is also important to be attentive to their marital and professional status."[22] (Document's emphasis)

Kate:
"I find I have to get in touch with myself."

> "My sense of this whole project though is...how we're affected by the catechesis, and what we're doing in that area; with the material we're receiving in the course, and our interactions with the children and how we're reflecting on that. So I don't see it threatening that way...but I find if you just ask me, "Is anything going on?" I say 'nah,' and nothing will be either, unless I stop and ask myself some good questions. I find I have to get in touch with myself."

Although it represents a challenge for her, Kate welcomes the opportunity to participate in this process which she interprets as "analyzing what [is] resonating inside and how it is affecting [her]." Her preface to these words manifests her appreciation of analytical thought and research:

> "What Montessori did and what Sofia did with the children about research is to observe them. And they did incredible analysis and research from that. That's what they did when they figured out what it was that resonated deeply within the child."

It has been said that this "catechesis challenges adults to on-going formation."[23] In Kate's awareness of the need for observation and reflection, we get a glimmer of some of its inherent challenges.

Ruth:
The "ups and the downs"

"It's a lot clearer and just hearing Francesca speak right there, it became even more clear. Yes, the 'highs and

Chapter Two: Adults: Two Companions

the lows', I understand that. It's not an easy journey."

Characteristically succinct, Ruth's few words nevertheless contain much weight. In response to a previous question as to the various "capacities" in which these catechists serve, her work involved every aspect, with the additional mention of areas such as "clean up, maintenance and supplies."

Behind these words is a general challenge which has been expressed this way: "A well-equipped atrium…challenges the creativity of those who furnish the space."[24] And, in the case of Ruth, that is in addition to the course and atrium sessions, as well as her familial and professional responsibilities. Later she will make reference to the "stress" this entails, thereby alerting us to another key consideration in the formation of catechists:

> "Always and in every way, lay catechists should be *recognized, respected, and loved* by their priests and communities. They should be supported in their formation and encouraged and helped to accomplish a task which is indispensable but far from easy."[25] (Document's emphasis)

Mary:
"It can be so mysterious."

"[It] can be so mysterious. [In] other children's programmes you certainly don't have to have any previous credentials, training or background, or anything else. Here [at my parish] they say, 'You have to have had all the preparation in order to be part of it [the atrium].' I think there is a bit of scepticism on some people's part. They don't really understand that and it [CGS] isn't something that shouts its own name either. So that even an observer [visiting the atrium] may not really completely understand what goes into it…"

At the end of our small group journey, Mary expresses her appreciation for the catechesis: "Life is so crazy now.[I] don't always succeed in slowing down as much as [I] would like, but it [CGS] keeps [me] in that direction. It's like this pull…"

Generally, Mary appreciates the focus of our small group. As she says, "it really enables us to help ourselves". Nonetheless, here Mary puts her finger on the question of the "preparation" required in this approach to ministry with children. Thus she identifies another challenge implicit in the CGS, which Mark Searle expressed as follows:

> "It's very difficult for people in our culture to look at this as something more than another idea of how to get things across to kids… It's about how a teacher sits with a child under the word of God or before the sacramental signs in an atmosphere of prayer… I feel very strongly that there's something fundamentally right about an approach which gives children the stories and vocabulary of the Christian tradition and does so in such a way that they feel themselves personally addressed by God."[26]

Domenica:
"I didn't think I fit into the group."

"The way that I come in with the children and just observing them and helping out if I can, I'm experiencing, really, a lot of what they're experiencing. I might be thinking different things than they are though, or I might just be acknowledging it just like they are… That's why I didn't think I fit into the group

Chapter Two: Adults: Two Companions

because I thought, I've never presented these materials. I'm learning as I am observing with the children a lot of the new materials or the presentations. So I'm just like the kids, taking it all in and going 'Wow' and enjoying it and receiving it with joy, just like the kids do. Meanwhile I'm observing them and their responses, but I'm also feeling the same things."

Domenica's question concerning her suitability in terms of this small research group stems mostly from her inexperience with children at this age. Nevertheless, her reference to the "new materials…presentations" implies a recognition of a particular challenge in this catechesis:

> "The catechist occupies an unusual place in this method. Less a teacher who imparts knowledge…the catechist becomes a fellow pilgrim, who journeys in the company of children who announces the message of another and has no claim to its effect."[27]

As well, Domenica's words about making the effort to "take it all in" indicate another inherent but challenging aspect of this catechesis. That is the need for openness and willingness to learn from children. Or, to phrase it another way, to be led by children:

> "The catechesis…asks us to learn from children, to be guided by them and to provide for their needs… The Catechesis of the Good Shepherd is led by the child. It is no wonder that it suits all children."[28]

Wendy:
"This is so different for me…"

"What I'm scared of [is] the research part of the work.

I don't want it to be held up under a microscope by somebody at university…It's a sacred thing to watch a child…and I appreciate the fact that I can see that because they seem transformed somehow… But I just feel like something new is starting within us that's going to affect all of us in a certain way. I have faith that it's going to benefit us… I've worked in the business world for twelve years and this is so different for me as a person to just come into a place where the work is so communal, so Christian…'

Wendy's words reflect the manner in which each catechist represents a different level of entry into our small research group. As the newest to this catechesis among us, it is understandable that Wendy experiences such feelings.

There is a deeper significance to Wendy's reservations. She is pointing to a challenging aspect implicit in this approach to children: "It's a sacred thing to watch a child." This is connected to some of her other references to children. For example, in watching children in the atrium, she explains: "There are no words for that for me". She adds: "It's not like that anywhere else, it's just in there [the atrium]", because "that love" seen in children "is powerful." Moreover Wendy, in words like these, indicates another challenge in this catechesis. That is, the implicit understanding that "children's spirituality is not just a matter of absorbing the faith of adults; it is a personal response to the indwelling God. Children have their own spiritual lives."[29]

The call, commitment and challenge in this catechesis, as seen from the viewpoint of the seven catechists, provide a concrete base upon which to explore some theoretical underpinnings of this catechesis. This is the subject of the next chapter.

Chapter Three:
Children: A "Different Way of Being Christians"

> Because there is in the child,
> there is in childhood a unique grace,
> An entirety, a firstness
> That is total.
> An origin, a secret, a spring, a point of departure,
> A beginning which might be called absolute.
> Children are new creatures.[30]

Generally speaking, every catechesis is based on a certain approach to God and to the human person as well. There is a dimension specific to this catechesis: the vision it holds of the child. It is an important element in relation to adults who accompany children, especially because, as Dr. Maria Montessori states: "If you have not got a vision of the child's soul, you cannot help in its development."[31]

We will look briefly at the spirituality of this catechesis on a pastoral level. Before doing so, however, there are two fundamental points to note. The first is that;

> "There is something peculiar about childhood that makes it difficult for anyone to think straight about it. We have all of course been children once, and that alone is enough to stock us with a powerful set of presuppositions, to make us all feel we know something about the subject."[32]

Therefore we will address some fundamental presuppositions in this catechesis.

The second point is the profound insight that Sofia learned from her work with children. With respect to the spiritual lives of children, Sofia maintained that "fundamentally—it would seem— it is about a different way of being Christians."[33] Thus we will allude to the approach to God and the child (the *who*), the content (the *what*), and the methodology (the *how*) in this catechesis.

Part 1: Spirituality of Childhood

*"I have come so that they may have life,
and have it in all its fullness."* (John 10:10)

On the pastoral level, the catechesis contains theological and educational presuppositions, along with basic psycho-pedagogical principles. We will look at some of the major ones associated with this catechesis, drawing mainly on the work of Dr. Maria Montessori and Sofia Cavalletti.

The child is a central paradox in Christianity: it is the littlest who are the greatest; if we are to receive the Kingdom of God we must become like a child (Matthew 18:3-4). An aspect of this paradoxical quality of childhood is captured by G. K. Chesterton who observed these two facts about children: "First, they are very serious, and secondly, that they are in consequence very happy." He adds: "The gravity of the very young child…is the gravity of astonishment at the universe."[34]

These are two qualities that characterize the spiritual lives of children. They have important implications for the religious growth of children. First, children are hungry for God. Feeding their hunger is a serious concern: "Children not

Chapter Three: Children: A "Different Way of Being Christians"

only have religious capacities but a particular hunger as well. When a child is hungry, he or she must be fed now, without waiting until tomorrow."[35] Second, children have the potential to encounter God. Actualizing their potential generates joy in them. As Sofia states:

> "The constant and repeated manifestations of joy children show in their relationship with God inclines me to say that the "image" of God, which is in all of us (Genesis 1:26), is reflected with a special transparency in children."[36]

Thus, in accompanying children along their religious path, we are invited into the child's way with God, which is to emphasize that:

> "There are no *ordinary* people... This does not mean that we are to be perpetually solemn. We must play. But our merriment must be of that kind (and it is, in fact, the merriest kind) which exists between people who have, from the outset, taken each other seriously."[37] (author's emphasis)

In the case of the child's religious development, Maria Montessori stresses the need to "respect the child's own religious life" and to recognize "its lofty seriousness."[38]

"Merely" Servant

What is said above implies the need to serve (*diakonia*) the God-child relationship. To return to the analogy of the child's hunger, it is obvious that the food provided to children directly influences their physical health, present and future. Generally, the younger the child, the more determining this influence is. This is just as true in terms of the child's religious formation.

That is, what is given, or not given, significantly affects the child's harmonious growth as a whole person, both now and later in life as well. Thus this can have long-term ramifications, either positively or negatively:

> "The Christian spiritual path is based on a deepening trust in God… Because trust is so important, our spiritual journey may be blocked if we carry negative attitudes toward God from *early childhood*…which are implanted in us largely as a result of early religious training…"[39] (emphasis mine)

In helping the relationship between the child and God to be established, we serve this relationship as "merely" servants, as stated in the Gospel of Luke 17: 10. Other translations use variations such as "unworthy", "useless", "unprofitable" servants.

Now if we extend the analogy, on a physical plane it is evident that the child is born with the physiological apparatus and mechanisms required to digest the food crucial for survival and growth. On the religious plane, however, it is not easily discernible that the young child is equipped with all the essentials necessary to receive and internalize the nourishment necessary to assuage his or her inner hunger and thirst.

First and foremost among these essentials are the child's capabilities for giving and receiving love: "in this covenant relationship with God, children find what is most precious in themselves: the capacity to love."[40]

Covenant Relationship

We know from scripture that only God can love immeasurably, for "God is love" (1 John 4:8). It is only God's love that can

Chapter Three: Children: A "Different Way of Being Christians"

completely satisfy the child's need for love without limits.

We also know from scripture, as St. Paul maintains, that no one can come to know who God really is without being told (Romans 10:14). Therefore, children need our help if they are to hear the good news of the Christian message (*kerygma*). Sofia expressed it this way:

> "Christianity is above all an event. Children cannot know that Christ died and is risen if they are not told and they need to know this."[41]

There is a request the child makes of us, even though it is unspoken in the early years: "Help me to come close to God. Help me to be fully who I am."[42] When children are helped in their relationship with God, their response is joyful: "I dare say…each time the child allows us to see the joy that she/he feels in drawing near to God…the child is allowing us to see his/her response to the God of the covenant."[43]

The Child's Way

There is something of an urgency in responding to this silent call of children, in so far as the childhood years are the most formative in one's life. What is experienced at this time has a radical impact. This is particularly the case in relation to the child's religious formation, understood as comprising all the potencies of mind and heart, body and spirit: "For the child, God is not a 'stop-gap God', as Bonhoeffer phrases it, but someone to whom one goes in the fullness of one's whole person."[44]

Yet, this is a delicate service because as Sofia states, "children seem to want to point out to us that *their* way of going to God is different."[45] (author's emphasis) It involves introducing children to scripture and liturgy in a way that helps children to experience their own personal encounter with God, independent of the adult. Thus children need to be given direct access to age-appropriate means of actualizing their encounter. Additionally, in offering children the proclamation of the Christian message, first and foremost we are called to be listeners to the Word of God together with the children:

> "Listening in community is always enriching. Listening with children is especially so, in our estimation, because God's Word resounds in a different manner in young children than in adults, and thus it is through children that another nuance of the Word reaches us. This will happen, however, on the condition that the catechist [has] the attitude of one who is open to listening…"[46]

Method: Incarnational Approach

This is why signs occupy a predominant place in this catechesis. Signs provide the essential instrument, such as biblical images and words, and liturgical symbols and gestures. Even the prepared space (atrium) and special objects (materials) share in this sign-quality. Indeed, Sofia characterizes this catechesis as a "method of signs," that method which

> "always remained alive where the life of the Church is living, and that is in the Liturgy. The Liturgy has always spoken through 'signs'; and Jesus taught only 'in parables' (Mark 4:34)."[47]

Therefore our service as catechists entails presenting signs in their most tangible form, as required by the different age groups of children. The sign is incarnated, so to speak, in the concretized form of biblical-liturgical materials. For example, the wooden figures representing the elements of the Good

Chapter Three: Children: A "Different Way of Being Christians"

Shepherd parable. In this way the sign's inherent power to captivate the child is further enhanced, and allows the child an immediate, first-hand experience. For this reason, an integral aspect of the catechist's service is to prepare and present these materials that "incarnate" these themes /signs, which thereby give the child access to a direct and personal experience of God.

Moreover, in this way children are enabled to meditate on the Christian message contained in the sign in a manner that involves them wholly. That is, children immerse themselves with all their faculties—physical as well as relational, cognitive as well as affective. This is also why the positive resonance generated by these themes can continue, in a different key, beyond the present experience to extend into the later stages of the child's life.

Content: Biblical and Liturgical Themes

The following is a very short synthesis of some of the pivotal biblical-liturgical "generative themes" that call forth such resonance in young children (3-6 years) and older children (6-9 years). "Generative themes" is a term employed by Thomas Groome. It is used here because Groome refers specifically to the work of Sofia in explaining what he means by "generative theme." For example:

> "...the generative theme signals to participants, and from the beginning, the vital core of the curriculum to be attended to... Then it functions akin to what Sophia [sic] Cavalletti, in her Montessori approach to religious education, calls a 'linking point.' By this she means 'an especially striking element that emphasizes the vital nucleus of the theme. The linking point

should introduce us into the heart of the subject in such a way that is gives us, in a flash, the global intuition of the essence of the subject we are considering.' The generative theme then should be of life import to participants, pertain to their very 'being' in place and time..."[48]

For children around the age of three to six, some of the generative themes are:

1) Christ the Good Shepherd knows and calls us by our own name (John 10); gives us his very life (in Baptism); and desires to meet us in a most particular way in the Eucharist.

2) God's life is within us (Christ, the light). It is so powerful that it permeates the entire created world (parables of the seed and the leaven (Matthew 13:31-33); and is given to us as a precious gift of inestimable value (parables of the pearl and the treasure, Matthew 13:44-46).

For children around the age of six to nine, some of the generative themes are:

1) Christ the True Vine invites us to share in the inexpressible intimacy of the Trinity (John 15); immerses us in God's cosmic plan of love; and calls forth our unique contribution in the building of the history of God's kingdom (Ephesians 1:10).

2) We are empowered to do this by God's presence and action in our lives (especially in the Eucharist), and God's constant love for me personally (experienced particularly in the sacrament of Reconciliation).

Chapter Three: Children: A "Different Way of Being Christians"

Summary

Across their long years of working with children, Sofia and Gianna discovered that what strikes the deepest chord in the young child is relationship--to be "known" and "called by name." This gives the child the reassurance of safety and protection. Even more, in the relationship with God young children gradually discover their identity and dignity as a "partner" in God's covenant. This is a primary descriptor of young children in Sofia's writings.[49] As she explains further: "In the covenant relationship the child finds the Partner who is limitless, unfailing love, who meets the child's deepest need, and the child is in harmony with the world."[50]

The children that the catechists speak about here (six to nine years) are at the age when they desire to explore new moral, intellectual and social horizons. They are "thirsty for a great vision," as Maria Montessori states.[51] Their fundamental need is for a steadfast, unchanging love, a love that never fails:

> "I have loved you with an everlasting love; therefore I have continued my faithfulness to you." (Jeremiah 31:3)

In this kind of relationship with God the older child discovers a new identity and dignity as a "collaborator" in the covenant. This is a dominant theme in Sofia's writings about older children: "The older child wants to know what his/her place is in the world that he or she is in the process of discovering, and what his/her task is in it."[52] Sofia adds however, that before attention is given to the level of doing—the "task," we must first attend to the level of "being"—the relationship. In other words, first we need to attend to the questions that the older child is asking us, even though they are not expressed explicitly: "Tell me with whom I do it, for whom I do it, with whom I am in relationship."[53] In other words, the foundation, first and foremost, is the covenant relationship with God. We will take a brief look at this in the next chapter.

Chapter Four:
Being in Love

"Childhood is the time for...being in love. Being in love is the essential foundation..."[54]

In looking at some of the pastoral and pedagogical aspects basic to this catechesis, we have seen that the principle dynamic in religious formation is the reality of relationship. Now we will open the framework for a moment's look into the religious reality itself, and especially as it relates to children.

The first two parts of this chapter take a brief look at the theological base. We do this by bringing two recognized theologians, whose works offer a rich perspective on religious experience, into dialogue with Sofia Cavalletti and Maria Montessori. Part three is a summary of Sofia's biblical understanding of childhood. It offers profound insights into the *why* behind this catechesis.

Part 1: Religious Experience

For our purpose here, it is important to frame the dialogue in its most generic context of the religious reality in itself. The work of the Canadian Jesuit, Fr. Bernard Lonergan (1904-1984), helps to open the horizons.

Fr. Lonergan begins his discussion on religion with the essential question of being in love with God: "Being in love with God, as experienced, is being in love in an unrestricted fashion." Lonergan is speaking here of the covenant relationship in its so-called vertical dimension: "For falling in love is a new beginning, an exercise of vertical liberty in which one's world undergoes a new organization."[55] According to Sofia, this is also the fundamental question in the religious development of children: "The necessary humus is the knowledge of a reality that draws me, a reality where I experience being loved and I love in return. The necessary humus…is always being in love."[56]

Religious experience is essentially the experience of relationship. In biblical language it is called the covenant relationship. God creates a covenant relationship with the child. Sofia writes,

> "the baptism of infants is a part of the most ancient tradition of the Church. This practice implies a recognition of the child's capacity to live in relationship with God, even from the time of infancy."[57]

Thus God is in relationship with the child from the beginning of life. The younger the child is however, the more mysterious that bond appears. Although this bond is not readily observable in young children, nonetheless, as Maria Montessori emphasizes:

> "the child must be permitted to penetrate into his supernatural life in his own peculiar manner. Even in the presence of God the child must remain a child."[58]

Therefore, to help the child "establish a relationship of being in love with God" is the fundamental task for the adult who accompanies children on their spiritual journey.[59] For this reason, Sofia insists, before we tell children "what to do," the child must be invited and allowed "to fall in love; and falling in love takes time." [60] The fact is that the child's relationship with God is lived interiorly and often remains unverbalized. This means that an attentive attitude on the adult's part is necessary:

The educator should, therefore, ascertain most minutely what are the circumstances and conditions—inside and outside the child—most favourable to the opening up of the child's soul to supernatural influences, to the vigorous and lasting co-operation with the grace of God.[61]

Part 2: Theology of Childhood

What has been said up to this point implies a theology of childhood. This is addressed in the work by the German Jesuit, Fr. Karl Rahner (1904-1984), called "Ideas for a Theology of Childhood."

> "In the intention of the Creator and Redeemer of children what meaning does childhood have, and what task does it lay upon us for the perfecting and saving of humanity?"[62]

With this question Rahner opens wide the frontiers of ministry with children. His first way of responding to it is to advocate the eternal value of childhood, against the too-common misconception of childhood as a solely provisional, preparatory state subordinate to adulthood.

He attests that divinely revealed scripture and Christian tradition attribute an unsurpassable, unique, and unrepeatable value to childhood. To these he adds the force of his own poetic voice. He depicts childhood as "a field which bears fair flowers and ripe fruits such as can only grow in *this* field and in no other, and which will themselves be carried into the storehouses of eternity."[63] (author's emphasis). Reinforcing and developing this image, Rahner continues:

> "The strange and wonderful flowers of childhood are *already* fruits in themselves, and do not merely rely for their justification on the fruit that is to come afterwards."[64] [emphasis mine]

This has important practical implications in accompanying children on their spiritual journey. For example, according to Montessori:

> "The educator who does not believe that children feel the truths of faith in a somewhat different manner from adults, and who does not realize that children need other ways than ours to express their hope and their love for God—such a one will not be able to guide the child in a manner suitable to his religious needs."[65]

The second way Rahner answers his question is to explore what scripture and tradition say about the Christian experience of childhood. Here we find what can be seen as the basic dialectic in terms of the ministry with children.

On the one hand, he maintains that scripture, especially the references he makes to certain passages in the New Testament and St. Paul, almost always presupposes we understand what a child is. Therefore it is left to us to determine what a child is from our own experience, even though we know this experience of ours is shadowy, complex and conflicting.

On the other hand, he states that the Christian understanding and experience of childhood as presented by Jesus is both realistic and idealistic at the same time. It is idealistic without glorifying childhood. It is realistic without failing to recognize the limits and insufficiency of childhood. However, as he maintains,

> "this does not mean that the "little ones" are lightly

estimated by Jesus in accordance with the attitude prevailing among his people and at his time."[66]

Christians, as Rahner points out, are not exempt from relegating children to a position inferior to that considered their due in the words of Jesus:

> "Now it is precisely the Christian above all who seems to lay special emphasis on the merely subordinate role of childhood, this character which it bears as preparation for the life that is to come, by comparison with the stage of adult life, which in consequence seems to be understood as life in the true sense."[67]

Part 3: The "Child as Parable"

This leads us to Sofia's exegetical work on the Gospel texts relating to children, entitled "The Child as Parable."[68] It is vital to include it here because

> *"the texts on Jesus and the children are difficult to understand...* Moreover, a superficial reading will not reveal that the very heart of the Christian Gospel is expressed in Jesus' gestures and sayings in relation to children."[69] (author's emphasis)

The second reason for including it is because this seminal work of Sofia's contains a radical vision of the child, which is at the very foundation of the catechesis. For these reasons it will be condensed here into the following five points.

A) There are two series of Gospel passages concerning children.

    1) The first series of Gospel passages is: Matthew 19:13-15; Mark 10:13-16; and Luke 18:15-17. In this first

series, all the synoptic texts include Jesus' insistence on letting the children come to him. Added to this, in Mark and Luke, is the passage about receiving the kingdom like a child, hence putting forth the child as an exemplar.

2) The second series of Gospel passages is: Matthew 18:1-6; Mark 9:33-37; and Luke 9:46-48. Sofia considers this second series to be more pertinent in relation to the child's parabolic character for two reasons. One is for the context in which these passages about the child occur: between the miracle of the possessed boy and the prediction by Jesus of his passion and resurrection. The other is for the exhortation these passages contain. That is, not only is the child to be welcomed, but to receive a child is tantamount to receiving Christ himself, and thus also the One who sent him.

B) Then the biblical theme of contrast is highlighted. This is found in these Gospel passages in these different forms:

little/great

first/last

   servant

great/the one who makes oneself little[70]

Each of these opposite poles is present in the child. For example, it is the fact of the littleness of children that establishes them as great in the kingdom of God. Sofia refers to other places in the teaching of Jesus where this contrast is to be found, especially in its parabolic form, such as the mustard seed, yeast, and grain (Mark 4:28), Sofia isolates one particularity. In these kingdom parables the relationship is "diachronic." For example, the mustard seed *is* the smallest and *will* be great. Whereas in the child, the relationship is "synchronic": the little child *is* greatest precisely because the child *is* littlest. Therefore, as Sofia clarifies:

> "There is no need to look into the far distant future to grasp the child's greatness, as in the case of the mustard seed. It is necessary, however, to be attentive to the greatness in the present littleness, to know how to see the power, already present and active, within it."[71]

C) Then two passages from St. Paul's second letter to the Corinthians are examined: 2 Corinthians 12:9-10; and 2 Corinthians 4:7.

Both these texts in St. Paul present a similar juxtaposition of two apparently irreconcilable elements which are fused synchronically together. As such, they shed an important light on Jesus' words about children.

In the first text there is Paul's experience of God's power working within his weakness: "power is made perfect in weakness…" (2 Corinthians 12:9-10). In the second text there is Paul's self-description: an earthen vessel containing a treasure (2 Corinthians 4:7).

Sofia sees this first passage from St. Paul as the "programmatic enunciation of the paradox of Christianity," and as expressing "perhaps *the* foundational motif, throughout all of Scripture." As well, the Gospel texts about children acquire another meaning in light of this passage. The child, whose weakness is a sign of strength, manifests a disconcerting reality:

"the paradox of the coexistence of littleness/greatness, powerlessness/power...that paradox which Christ will live to the utmost in his Death and Resurrection."[72]

D) The effect of this insight is heightened further. Now Sofia examines the context in which this second series of texts occurs: the miracle preceding the passage about the child, and the death/resurrection prophecy following it. All three are seen as interlinked and united.

Jesus, in order to help the apostles grasp what they were unable to hear about his passion, resorts to a parable, his habitual teaching method (Matthew 13:34). At this all-important moment, however, Jesus chooses a human parable, the child—in whose weakness and littleness is the greatest. The child is a living example of what Jesus is proclaiming, namely, that the power and victory that would be his in rising would happen by suffering through the greatest weakness: death.

This, in turn, deepens the meaning of Jesus' identification with and affinity for children: "whoever receives one such child in my name welcomes me" (Mark 9:37). For as it is in Christ, so too is it in children that God's power is revealed in weakness.

E) This reflection ends with an invitation.

If it is true that the child is a parable, then, like all parables, the child is composed of two elements. One element is visible—littleness. The other element is hidden and mysterious—greatness. In the child, as in all parables, these two elements are inseparable. And, as with all parables, we are summoned to look beyond appearances:

Chapter Four: Being in Love

> "If it were justifiable to make a distinction among the virtues which express the foundational religious attitude in its three different aspects, we could say that the mustard seed is an object of hope, the child is an object of faith."[73]

In the framework of this vision of the "child as parable," perhaps catechesis can be seen not only as a ministry to or *with* children, but also as a ministry of children. We catch glimpses of this in the following chapters.

Chapter Five:
The the Sources

We begin our exploration of the catechists' relationship with God as it emerged through their accounts of the encounter with God in sacred scripture (part one) and liturgy (part two).

Part 1: Word of Life: Bible

In encountering God through scripture, the parable assumes a pre-eminent place for the catechists. A common characteristic is the affective level of engagement that the parable elicits in them. Their references to parables are usually accompanied with a noticeable feeling level. The following are some of their responses.

Parable

Mary reflects on the particular impact of the parables of the Good Shepherd and True Vine (Gospel of John, chapters 10 and 15).

> "The presentations are beautiful—the very gentle introduction of the moral aspect is so perfect. The interweaving of the two images of shepherd and vine is so powerful in conveying what our God is like."

Here the parable's impact is due to its "image" content. The image resonates deeply, thus powerfully communicating the presence of God.

Chapter Five: The Sources

Ruth's response to hearing parables is expressed as excitement: "Hearing the vine being continually linked to the Greater Being is exciting." Later, in the same meditation, she states forcefully: "The parable is very powerful to me. The <u>love</u>, the <u>life</u> surging through every part of the <u>total</u>."[74]

For Wendy, the parable is a particularly rich source of nourishment. It is also an entranceway into mystery for her, and points to the time when all will be revealed:

> "I believe that this is part of the mystery of Christ working in us. He is sharing himself with us, though our hunger to know him as he really is, is not completely satisfied. Especially in the parables, he is saying to me that I will know "the rest" in Heaven."

Domenica reflects on certain parts of the True Vine parable, such as "fruit," "to remain…" This stirs the memory of something her daughter sang after receiving First Eucharist:

> "A's [daughter] song she sang to me, '*Vieni Gesù – resta con me, resta con me, e non lasciarme più.*" More verses, I don't know them."

The words of this Italian song, "remain with me and never leave me," refer to the moment in the Emmaus journey with the risen Christ. The two disciples urged Jesus, "Stay with us, because it is almost evening, and the day is now nearly over" (Luke 24:29). The actual song is a prayer that the Lord remain with *us*. Interestingly, however, Domenica has written it in the first person: "remain with *me*.[75] Then she indicates that joy is the special "fruit" this parable brings, and links it to the joy she felt at an earlier time when hearing her daughter's song:

> "The fruit is the joy—a scene after my daughter received her First Holy Communion."

Like Leaven

The joy that Domenica experiences now during the course appears as a definitive moment. She will speak of it seven months later as a privileged and surprisingly "deep" experience. While this will be referred to in more detail later, it is important to note the enduring quality of this experience. What is sparked during an encounter with scripture (parable) in Spring becomes a moment that remains vivid for many months to follow. This deeply felt experience of encounter does not disappear as a fleeting moment, but lingers and is recalled much later.

Finally, Mary's terse statement emphasizes the universality contained within the parable's limitless boundaries:

> "The richness drawn from the parable; that it is difficult to tell where the vine and branch begin and end, that there is a place on the vine for all people."

The parable is pre-eminent in the catechists' reflections also because it opens to them the Bible as a whole, connecting the Hebrew and Christian scriptures together. Ruth writes:

> "The Old Testament sources for the True Vine [parable]—I was amazed at the richness of the depth of their meaning in the early ages. That the simple parable that we are presenting to children has great meaning."[76]

Ruth identifies certain themes in the parable and their affective resonance for her:

> "'Remain in my love.' 'No one has ever reflected human love as Christ has shown.' With these two phrases, I would just 'be.' There is great comfort and security with these words."

Domenica also expresses a feeling-laden response:

> "The idea of the pruning of the vines, and creation being renewed, from the book of Genesis—made me think that just as nature is renewed, in each season we too are being renewed in our relationship, in our love of God."

Further, she alludes to the nature of scripture as an inexhaustibly rich source of personal sustenance:

> "Hearing over and over again that God loves us, wants a constant union and communion with us, brings so much joy to my soul. [It] renews my spirit with the strength of his unchanging love. [It] renews my belief and faith in our partnership. No matter how much I hear about God's love for us, I can't get enough of his message."

Scripture as Integrating

Scripture has the power to effect an integration between the biblical source and personal experience. Mary singles out the aspect of "revelation" in relation to the evangelical sayings of Jesus. In this catechesis we refer to these sayings with the word *maxims*.[77] As well, there is an allusion to children in the atrium. She points to the personal-ministerial interplay in the scriptural encounter. Mary's excerpt also exemplifies how the presence of children pervades the encounter even when they are not physically present:

> "The maxims as God's gifts, as His revelations, so we may be happy and grow and know His confidence is in us. The children will most certainly love these words as I love them."

In the next excerpt, Eileen indicates the integrative aspect of listening to scripture in the course, specifically in its relation to catechesis with children:

> "In preparing to make these announcements to children, we steep ourselves in the theology of the proclamation, which would be enough already. But then, the experience with children is able to draw us to perhaps the most important or [to] simply explore, enjoy and give thanks for the gifts that are boundless."

Scripture as Consoling

The affective impact of scripture comes in an explicit form of consolation. Wendy reflects on the biblical understanding of the parousia. It is linked to two important dimensions in her encounter with God, namely, mystery and emotion:

> "Our final destination of Parousia is revealed to us while remaining in powerful mystery, and affirms itself too. I believe the Catechesis draws each catechist out as each is drawn inward, toward their own individual spirit. Jesus wishes that his light be revealed to all nations, that this flame will warm all hearts."

The feeling element in the encounter with scripture is also clear in the following excerpt from Domenica's reflection on the maxims:

> "Following the <u>will of God's heart</u>—deep felt emotion. Commandment of God to us in Torah—God is disclosing to us his nature. Maxims—tie in to above—what is very dear and deep in Jesus' heart. —new way of being and doing."

Chapter Five: The Sources

Scripture as Provocative

Scripture provokes as well as consoles. Kate reflects on the biblical presentation/material for children on "The unity of the History of the Kingdom of God."[78] It spurs Kate to confront the world's harsh realities in the light of the Gospel message of resurrection:

> "I love this presentation—it's so visual, so tactile—imagining thousands of years flowing through our fingers!! And it's so hopeful. When I think that we have the risen life in us, that we have the benefit of God being made human and walking amongst us and then I look at the atrocities we as a society commit…I can be totally deflated. But putting this into the perspective of time gives me hope. Reading Scripture makes me feel, I think, that the end time is just around the corner (I guess that's the best way to get us to "shape up"), but when we see how long it's taken to prepare all this for us and how relatively little time we've had to transform it and even littler [sic] time to experience the risen life of Christ, well there's hope!"

Scripture as Transforming

Francesca's meditation on the same biblical theme manifests the transformative quality in scriptural sources. The experience of listening to scripture draws forth from Francesca a deeply personal reflection. She is struggling with difficult personal issues—"the good and the bad times"—in the light of the biblical revelation that "creation is on–going". Viewed in the vastness of salvation history, there is hope in her struggle. This hope includes an opening to others in the larger community. It is also linked to the insight that the True Vine parable created within her earlier during the course. Noteworthy is the recurrence of a receptive-responsive combination that is a commonality in her encounter with God through scripture:

> "It's great to hear "creation is ongoing." Not everything is set. While I try to let God breathe into me, I am becoming a new creation. A creation for him, his glory, his love. That is when I remember! We fit on the time line as individuals, not just as a moment. Not just as a series of holy sacred moments of sacraments on a time line but the good and the bad times mixed together going towards Parousia. Time in God's time, in God's breath, in God's universe, in God's plan. I don't want to run so much. Where would I go? I'll remain on the vine, in the plan, in the breath, in love—never alone."

This excerpt is the second reflection Francesca devoted to the theme: "creation, redemption and parousia." This encounter with God, sparked by the theme of the one, unified plan of God will endure over time. Francesca will continue this inner dialogue for months afterwards, as will be seen later. This moment, recorded in June, marks the initiation of a prayer-meditation that she will refer to in September as the most valuable aspect of the whole experience. Later she relates:

> "It began with the whole "creation" thing; when meditating about this, it was like [I] actually got a gift out of it. The gift was a form of prayer. That's what I will always remember from that moment; not so much the First Communion [retreat] and all those things that happened, but this prayer…"

Chapter Five: The Sources

Part Two: Food of Life: Liturgy

Liturgy is as formative a source of encounter with God as scripture. We will see that the liturgy is also as multi-faceted as scripture in evoking response from the catechists.

The Power of Liturgy

After the course session on the Mass (Eucharistic Prayer IV), Kate reflects with enthusiasm:

> "the incredible words in the Liturgy hold so much meaning, it would take a lifetime to appreciate what they have to convey."

Her expression of appreciation then moves to a personal application, which manifests a marked level of self-awareness as well as humor:

> "As usual, I see the glass half empty (as opposed to half full)—instead of delighting in what I do know and understand, I am focused on my need to fill up that glass—on my need to understand these words and all that is connected to them."

Ruth highlights the power of the liturgy to evoke a response. She is captured by the "gestures of gift" in the Eucharistic rite: namely, the gesture of offering, exchange of peace, and the breaking of bread:[79]

> "I am moved by the imagery of the hands as the symbol of the child's gift—the Epiclesis, the Offering. Then, the Gift of Peace, so incredibly powerful, by joining hands, especially when it is equated to the Sap running through branches in the True Vine. The power of such

great love in the Risen Christ."

Significantly, Ruth is suggesting liturgy as an encounter with the risen Christ. Just as significant is her connection of the Bible (allusions to the True Vine parable) with liturgy (the Eucharistic rite: its signs and gestures). She also notes the impact of "imagery." That is, not only the symbolism contained in the parable (sap), but also the gestures-movement have a particularly forceful quality.

Liturgy as Living Encounter

This same course session on the Eucharistic Prayer is recorded by Domenica as an actual experience. What impressed Domenica about it was that it was not merely an "academic" study, so to speak, along with the gestures of gift (as presented to children). It was also a participatory experience in which the whole group was engaged:

> "As we each heard and partook in the reading of the Eucharistic prayer and as we sang the Holy, Holy, Holy and the Mystery of Faith, etc., I felt the harmony of our hearts together in faith and love and joy as we participated."

This session on the Eucharist, lived in a participatory way, led Domenica to consider her own experience of the Mass:[80]

> "Listening to Sofia's meditation on the Mystery of Faith fills me with awe and anticipation. I always believed that the people at Jesus' time were more fortunate because they heard and saw, but in retrospect we are more fortunate for we receive God's gift at every Mass that we attend."

Chapter Five: The Sources

In other words, delving into the liturgy stimulated her personal appreciation of the Eucharist.

Liturgy as Linked to Scripture

Mary's course journal had a reflection entitled, "Reconciliation Meditation," in which we can see a movement happening. It moves from an appreciation of the biblical understanding of "commandment," to an awareness that this represents a personal invitation, and then to a level of response:

> "I loved hearing that commandment is an expression of God's will, the plan of his heart. Also, that we are invited into the love that unites the Father, Son and Spirit—that this is where we are asked to remain. It is so wonderful…that the closer we get to the true meaning, the more wonderful it is—God never disappoints us."

Once again, the connection between Bible and liturgy is implicit—between scripture as it is proclaimed and lived (in Reconciliation). The final sentence reveals her realization of the unfailing nature of God's love.

Eileen makes reference to an additional source material relating to the liturgy of Reconciliation:[81]

> "My reaction/reflection focuses on Mongillo's comments on the reality of the breakdown of this relationship between God and person. When the need to draw closer is lessened or non-existent—signal the 'death' of this relationship."

Reflecting on this leads her to recognize the importance of what she terms "moments of encounter," an allusion to the sacrament of Reconciliation:

"The need for moments of encounter are then a strong need in light of this closeness that must be indeed experienced to be 'longed' for when there is separation."

Liturgy as Linked to Catechesis with Children

Liturgical theology (theory) has its pastoral application in catechesis with children (ministry). Francesca is reflecting on the presentation of the "Synthesis of the Mass."[82] She is personally struck by the sign or symbol—the language of the liturgy highlighted in the materials for this liturgical presentation with children. This awareness will then be applied to her ministry. Francesca begins:

> "To see the material again… How simple it looks, how easy… The first time I saw it I was dumbstruck. I was in awe, it was so beautiful, the hands, the lights, the crucifix. All was complete. I love this and I am glad it's familiar."

This reflection was written after the course (theoretical learning), but now she moves into its implication for her ministry:

> "I wonder if the children will want to move pieces around. I'll look back at this and freely let them."

After speculating about if and how the children will move these materials, she then arrives at very specific applications, such as changing one of the cards for the materials, etc. She then concludes:

> "The children will work with this material and love to go back to the altar in the 3 to 6 atrium and make the moment live again and again and again."

Wendy also illustrates the integration between theory and

Chapter Five: The Sources

practice. In her case, the spill–over works the other way: from the experience of catechesis (atrium) to liturgical theology (theory). First she relates what appears as an important insight to her:

> "As has been said about liturgy, how it brings the past into reality, makes it the present and the now."

Then she links a line in Sofia's book on liturgy to her ministry experience, and reflects:

> "I understand more and more why it is easy for me to romanticize the catechesis. The work is borne [sic] of love, in many shapes and forms. As Sofia wrote in <u>Liturgy</u>, God reveals himself to us, yet we cannot see him. So this love from God that has brought me to this place, makes me want to return again and again."[83]

"This place" Wendy is referring to is the atrium. It is noteworthy that when she is writing about her time in the atrium, she is recalled back to and appreciates the liturgical sources presented in the course.

Summary

"Welcome the word implanted in you that has power."
(James 1:21)

This chapter looked at the formation experience of the catechists in terms of the bible and liturgy as sources of encounter with God. The next chapter looks specifically at the encounter with God as mediated by means of the biblical and liturgical materials, and their mode of presentation, and how both help the adult's meditation and prayer.

Chapter Six:
Good News of Great Joy: The Christian Message

The biblical and liturgical materials are designed with the aim of helping the child's meditation and prayer, as we said. Now we look at these materials, and their mode of presentation, as a source of the adult's formation. That is, we discover how the materials which are intended for children may also mediate the adults' encounter with God.

The outline of the course themes given previously (chapter 1) provides the backdrop for the catechists' excerpts presented here. It is difficult for someone who has not seen the catechesis in action to appreciate the manner of verbal presentation and the way in which the materials are moved to concretize a biblical or liturgical theme.[84] Therefore, this chapter will offer glimpses into the impact these have on the catechists, and how they serve as a formative source for their relationship with God.

Part 1: Materials for the Message

As we proceed, headings are offered to single out some of the inner dynamics that appear to be occurring in the catechists as they reflect on their experiences.

Chapter Six: Good News of Great Joy: The Christian Message

Appropriation of Theoretical and Experiential Learning

Both the presentation and material for the Eucharist stir Eileen to appreciate the meaning of the Mass, as she states:

> "It struck me how much we all need this 'breaking down' of such complex, rich experiences. We are able to look at, enjoy, and meditate on each part of the Mass. How rich that the potential for every 'single' moment is great in regard to opening onto new horizons.

Eileen notes that this is also true for other sacraments ("Baptism"), as well as scripture ("the Parable").

The materials used for the Mass aid understanding and clarity. For example, they are a means of apprehending more about liturgy in a way that engages the adult in unexpected ways. For example, Mary writes:

> "I liked seeing the interchange of all the different elements of the Mass—of seeing the flow of the Mass laid out on one flat plane."

She then notes that it is a particularly rich liturgical presentation, and highlights its elucidating character:

> "The character of this presentation is so different from others we have heard recently—all these different facets that reveal the truth and clarify our understanding."

This cognitive experience has a unifying effect on Mary. She concludes:

> "The whole (Mass) seems so much more whole after putting together the pieces. The signs, symbols, and

prayers are so unified."

Ruth highlights the nature of the same material and presentation on the Mass as a means for deepening meditation. She notes:

> "I am very moved by the simplicity of the Mass presentation and how such simple things and words create such discussion."

Ruth also remarks on the maxim material: "As each phrase is presented, it provides more meditative 'need'." As that "need" is met, Ruth is encouraged to go deeper:

> "Having taught the maxims in a similar way for 2 years, I am now much more excited to meditate some more and now feel more centered as to the meaning and presentation style."

The excerpts show how the materials are a means of facilitating the movement from intellectual knowing to a more holistic experience. Or, to quote Kate's capsule comment: "The materials are a point of departure for reflection and <u>NOT</u> a point of arrival."

Invitation to Communion with God

The materials and presentations serve as a prism through which we can see the ways in which the adult approaches the encounter with God. For Domenica the materials evoke something different:

> "The honor and dignity of presenting the materials in this course is always amazing."

What is striking to her are the "tone, gestures, sensitivity to

Chapter Six: Good News of Great Joy: The Christian Message

the materials, and the group". All of these, she says, "touched me." She is "touched" to the point of opening to God: [85]

> "I enjoyed hearing and envisioning the flow of the moments of the True Vine presentation. It is probably the first time the children get to enjoy the presentation and with each moment get into it deeper because I enjoyed the revelation and the feeling of how close Jesus wants us to be to him. So close—the union is so vital, no separation between us."

We note again how the presence of children is felt in the course. That is, the catechists' atrium experience is central to their reflections even in their course journals.

Eileen probes the nature of the parable presentation. She indicates its value for the adult on various levels. She also indicates that experiencing the presentation in the manner that it is given to children acts as an antidote to the inevitable frustration that is found in the ministerial practice:

> "The value, struck me, of the need to hear the richness of the parable in very small 'doses' that settle like water into soil as one waters a plant. The water does not pool but is fully absorbed into the soil and to the roots. So, we must value and respect this method of slowness and essentiality with the child. I know that it requires much 'back planning' to allow for this time, and at times there is a sense of frustration when time is at a premium in regard to celebration."

The words "slowness" and "essentiality" are noteworthy here. Not only does the child have a need to experience this. It also helps the adult to receive the Word in "small doses" too.

Levels of Engagement: Personal, Pastoral and Practical

Eileen comments: "I enjoyed the dialogue that was brought forward through these materials." The materials not only generate discussion among the catechists. They also generate a multi-layered dialogue within themselves as individuals.

The following reflection by Francesca will be quoted at length for three reasons. The first reason is that ostensibly it is the material that has stimulated this multi-leveled reflection. The second reason is that it reveals the complexity and the richness of reflection it stirs. The third reason is that it indicates the interplay between the course (theory) and catechesis in the atrium (experience with children). With the materials as the departure point, one sees a flow back and forth from the catechist (in the course), to a movement toward children (in the atrium), then a movement back towards the catechist at a deeper level still. In quoting this reflection, we will simply note these different movements. They also give a preview to some of the other categories that will be dealt with further in the following chapters.

Francesca titles this reflection "Maxims". She begins by noting:

> "…wording about 'ties you to creation and recreation' was a major light. Yes, the world is the same, not much changes. People can change —> new creation. With Christ in me, I am better able to fulfill the maxims. This is being led by Christ—very exciting potential for me."

Then her meditation takes a turn toward the adult's role in ministering to children:

> "We should take time to meditate more on this with the children and share this in a community 'safe' experience for them, not primarily as witnessing but as being part of the process of remaining."

Now she considers the use of this material in the atrium: "I can see developing more material for follow-up...(This is for somewhat older children.)—this could be exciting!" At this point, Francesca's reflection moves to the consideration of children at a deeper level: "If we have trouble, anxieties, problems that lead us as adults [to] sin, then this is true for children too!" Further, in reflecting on Reconciliation and the mystery of sin, she moves to a personal application:

> "I feel like I'm a beginner at learning to let Jesus transform my life—not so that I stop sinning, but so that I can exercise options for revelation which attracts me more than the result of sin."

Here her reflection seems to have come full circle. Just as the evangelical sayings of Jesus (maxims) acted as a springboard for deeper meditation, now a "revelation" appears to her as an "attractive" prospect. It is interesting to see how simple wooden maxim plaques acted as the catalyst in this rich moment for her—"I feel like I am a beginner at learning to let Jesus transform my life."

Part Two: Meditation and Prayer

We have been given glimpses into a meditative dimension in these presentations on biblical-liturgical themes and the use of the materials which concretize them. At times this dimension leads into prayer. Since this is such a significant fact, a number of examples from the catechists' journal reflections will be presented here.

In writing about the liturgical presentation on the Mystery of Faith (in the Eucharistic rite), Mary ponders: "To imagine Parousia—it's something I would like to think about in a quiet moment." There is not only an inner stirring toward "imagining Parousia." There is also a drawing to reflect on it again during some quiet time, which is suggestive of prayer.

Invitation to Prayer

Kate's reflection relating to the materials for the "maxims" highlights another aspect. Her "analytical mind" begins to probe the meaning these maxims have for her personally: "Jesus leaves us with maxims—which are almost if not completely impossible, 'Love…as I have loved you', 'forgive 70 x 7'…" With her habitual honesty, she moves from an immediate feeling–response towards a deeper appropriation of the message contained in the maxims: "At first it feels very discouraging—to set goals so high makes me want to give up before I have even started. But then I receive the revelation that I can do this because of God's love for me!!" Her concluding words indicate openness and willingness, dispositions associated with prayer:

> "That never failing, abundant, unconditional, ever present flowing love which I need only receive empowers me, flows through me and out to the world, if only I allow it to. I only need say yes and it will be done. I only need to allow myself to be the instrument, the vessel to receive this treasure."

This reflection by Wendy occurred in a course session in which the theme of Reconciliation was addressed. What is interesting here is that while she is in the course, she is drawn back to the experience of the sacrament of Reconciliation in the atrium, which the children had just celebrated. This liturgical theme

Chapter Six: Good News of Great Joy: The Christian Message

sparks the memory of that experience with the children.[86] In this case, we can see that the experience with children influences the learning in the course, informing it with evident emotion. She begins by alluding to the celebration: "We recently celebrated our children's first Reconciliation in the atrium. It is an hour that became a moment, a moment still alive for me." She concludes with an expression of praise:

> "Memories of the atrium, like the word, are brought forward into reality. Many moments of the catechesis for me have been lived this way. Ever present and alive, as the vine. We see the flow of God's meanings and teachings to us. We are touched and enhanced by the reality that is in these moments, we experience Jesus being alive. Jesus is alive. He is risen. Alleluia."

As well, even attending the course offers a meditative opportunity for Wendy. At another time, she takes the time to reflect before the course session began. At the top of her journal page she notes, "This was written before class, as I had arrived early and often like to prepare for the evening by meditating."

Passage to Prayer

The next reflection by Ruth exemplifies the dialogue between oneself and God's Word as proclaimed and lived in the liturgy. Ruth reflects on the presentation of the Mystery of Faith after the course session. It is given here exactly as it was written. Even the structuring gives an impression of dialogue, with one voice heard, the other responding. It concludes with her summary comment on the experience:

> "I feel so much like a 'little' child hearing this. I can't wait for the next word, what is going to happen, where

my place in all this is. Jesus calls us to be close (I'm here) by our name (Wow). Over time, how many people know Jesus. <u>Imagine</u> the tone of his voice. (I can hear it.) Are these people lucky? (We are too.) We know more. Death. Risen. Jesus is truly there. Our eyes not strong enough to face the Splendour of the Resurrection (But when?). There will be a day!!! (Yes!!) There is such great wonder, expectation, excitement. I feel I am so much a part of this presentation. I can't wait to hear the next word. Tonight has been a great 'moment'."

A similar movement is seen in the following excerpt by Domenica. She wrote it after the session on the Eucharistic Prayer. It begins with her response to "the great Amen—our yes to God."[87] As in the previous reflection, one is reluctant to add any words, because it is an "I–Thou" encounter in an explicit form. God is being addressed as "you":

"Yes too I am here with you—in the Trinity togetherness—that's what we long for, is to always be together—in relationship, in celebration.

—How much you loved us, how much we mean to you.—Yes—I understand, I accept, I love you too, I also want to be a part of you.

—now I really understand—the meaning of this great Amen.

—What meaning this course has put to my words, understanding, love of God, knowledge of God's love for us.

—I keep on echoing—the aching, the longing, the yearning for God that this course has awakened in me through revelation—in words, in gestures, in respect, in dignity that is revealed."

Meditation and Prayer

The final selection speaks to what Francesca prized as the best "gift" of the small group process. It was initiated, as mentioned earlier, by the presentation of the history of the kingdom of God. Francesca's immediate response begins: "'Plan of love'. I'm so glad to re-hear that there is a plan to all this and God's plan is love!" The meditation is too long to reprint in full, and only its flow will be outlined here, inasmuch as it dominates her journal (with regard to impact as well as the amount of text it comprises).

First, there is a focus on God as Creator breathing life into Adam. Then there is a personal awareness: "I breathe. How much does God breathe life into me?" She continues to wonder, "Is every breath I take God breathing into me?" Going back in time to recall Adam, then coming back to her existential situation, she wonders about God's presence during times of "crisis, stress, illness, pain, rejection." From this arises the image of "Jesus, the Good Shepherd, [who] is our friend and is always with us", followed by the conviction that God does not "want to be with us in misery" only, but that God "is a God of love". At this point, she recognizes an opportunity: "I really should try to invite God to breathe into me more often. Perhaps everyday. Let God's breath come into me."[88]

The next day Francesca's meditation continues. Returning to her difficult life situation, she muses, "Can I change it by inviting God to breathe into me where it hurts the most? Can I change my life by inviting God to breathe into me like a new creation each day?" Her reflection lingers awhile on her attitudes, "What could happen? How would it feel?" She speculates about launching out in trust: "Do I trust God to be there for me in the good and bad—sounds like wedding vows."

From this note, her meditation touches on: Christ's life on earth and after his resurrection; the Pentecost period when "three to five thousand people were converted in one day"; and linking the action of God at creation in breathing life into Adam with the action of the Spirit of the risen Lord causing this "new explosion on earth". Then there is the movement into prayer. Francesca wonders if she should pray that the "explosive breath of God fill [her] life." Self-awareness—"I'm a little-lot afraid"—is followed by prayer: "May every breath I take be of God. He will fill it with the quality of air I need to sustain life." Finally, she offers a closing comment on the experience, expressing joy and discovery: "WOW. I sure didn't get this idea the first time I heard the words in other courses!"

The following week, Francesca's meditation on the revelation that "creation is ongoing", is now expressed in diagrammatic form. It is her "timeline" to represent her own version of salvation history about what "the breathing of God looks like." Many months and pages later, there comes the statement, "...a conclusion!" For brevity's sake, only two points will be noted about her conclusion to this prolonged meditative experience. The first point is that this experience does not remain within the orbit of her personal life alone. Instead, it concludes with a reference to children. The imagery in these few lines is evocative:

> "I think I'm like the 6-9 year old children. Seeds are planted and it takes a while for them to grow in us, we hear and see things, but our reactions are not completely spontaneous. It takes time for us to work

Chapter Six: Good News of Great Joy: The Christian Message

things through. (It took me all summer to get to this point.) I think I'll always honour the children's response of silence and work better because of the process I let myself go through."

The second point is the gratuitous effect of this experience as a whole: "I did not know where it was leading me, but I felt very directed and inspired by God. I pray that each breath I take will be an explosion creating new life in me. I am now more able to trust in God's plan and God's love." In these concluding words, a transformation process seems to be occurring by means of what she called at the start as the "gift of prayer".

As these excerpts already indicate, the presence of children appears to have a formative influence in the personal as well as ministerial lives of these catechists. Before turning to this subject in the next chapter, this diagram is offered as a synthesis of these last two chapters.

In the last chapter we explored the catechists' relationship with God in terms of the biblical and liturgical themes which serve as a source of encounter with God. In this chapter we highlighted the mediating function of the methodological elements. That is, the manner in which the presentation and use of the materials, designed for children, helped the catechists' to internalize the theological themes. Thus the combined effect of the content and method appeared to lead into meditation and prayer.

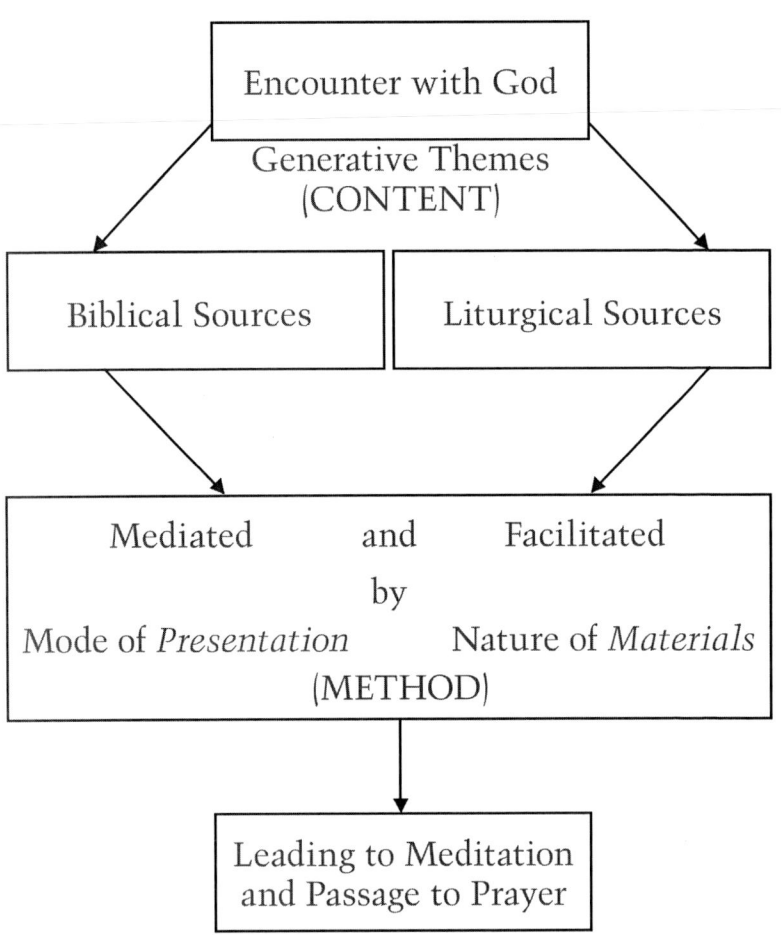

Figure 1

Chapter Seven:
The Formative Presence of Children[89]

As the catechists' excerpts have already indicated, there appears to be many ways in which children help them in their own formation. We explore only three aspects or sources of nourishment children offered them.

1) Celebrating and meditating with children.

2) The contribution that the atrium—as community and space—makes in relation to the quality of these encounters.

3) Some specific gifts which these catechists received in their ministry experience with children. These gifts manifest the manner in which they are nurtured by children both in their personal lives and pastoral ministry.

Part 1: Celebrating and Meditating with Children

Two elements of the experience of being in community with children seem to be of paramount importance for these seven catechists: a) celebrating and listening to God, and b) meditating together with children. These are the elements that are the focus of the following few excerpts.

Celebrating in Community with Children

Wendy writes succinctly about the special children's retreat during which the children celebrated the sacrament of

Reconciliation. She describes it as being a moment of great insight for her:

> "Children do not live 'time' as adults do. They live in the moment, never regretting or wondering. They move forward in life, with time, toward more time. They look forward to each moment, as it were...."

Wendy's account speaks of the retreat from the perspective of a catechist experiencing this for the first time with children in the atrium. The following excerpt by Kate, a long-time catechist, relates an experience of celebration that also happened during the sacramental retreat, one that seems directed by the children themselves. It is this fact, and the absorption and delight of the children during the celebration of the Word, that most strike Kate (initials represent the names of the children):

> **"Friday p.m. May 5.**
>
> —The children received their Bibles in the a.m. with total delight—S. [catechist] invited them to choose a favorite reading or story which they might read for our celebration of the Word in the afternoon—they all offered at least one story, some of them choosing the same story:
>
> The Last Supper: M.J. and T. [children's names]
>
> > The Good Shepherd: G. and A.
> > The Missing Sheep: J. and N.
> > Feeding of the Five Thousand: E. and O.
> > Daniel in the Lion's Den: L.
> > Catching the Fish
> > The True Vine: A. and O.
>
> They were very excited about reading the stories and

Chapter Seven: The Formative Presence of Children

took great delight in finding them in the Bible. Two people could not read: one of them memorized, 'This is my body—take it, eat it,' and 'This is my blood—take and drink it,' and she pretended to read the words at the appropriate time during the Last Supper account. The two girls doing the Feeding of the Five Thousand couldn't locate it in the Bible, so they wrote the story out on a piece of paper. When I located the story for them, they asked if they could read it from their Bibles (which is what, in fact, we were doing). Was it that the Bible seemed so precious, so sacred that they wanted to make sure they were allowed to read from it?

—The children were *very* attentive through our celebration—which was simply an opening and closing song and all their readings with an alleluia between each...."

Francesca is impressed by the child's capacity for celebration and their enjoyment in it. Here she presents a synthesis of her six years' experience of the children's First Eucharist and Reconciliation retreats. She notes the impact of these moments of celebration for the children, one that lasts well beyond the retreat itself. She begins, "this was our sixth retreat for children celebrating Reconciliation and First Communion." Then she comments on this overall experience with a hint of humor about any tendency toward idealism:

"In all I did not observe something different or new. There was no major revelation to me that somehow this retreat was any better than any other retreat we had done in our atrium. It is not in the individual moments and the things the children said or how they responded that confirms my belief that what we expose the children to during this retreat proves to me how important the themes [are that] we present to the children [and how they] touch their lives. BUT rather in their hunger before the retreat, the silence, joy and community of the retreat and the outpouring of their response long after the retreat is over. So I'm not going to give a series of beautiful statements said by the children during the times of our presentations of the themes of the Good Shepherd and the True Vine.

I will tell you that there were such profound moments of silence, peace, joy, trust, and meditation that at times it was all I could do not to burst into song, tears, laughter or spontaneous celebration."

Meditating Together with Children

The mention of "such profound moments of…meditation" leads to the second element that emerges with respect to communal moments with children. That is, the experience of meditating with children.

One journal account by Eileen indicates that communal meditation is nourishing for children: "Such quiet and full attention." Another speaks about a specific moment of meditating together with the children on the rite of Reconciliation:

> "Reconciliation.
> There was complete silence which was noticeable in the natural excitement of the day. Eyes were direct. The meditation spoke to them, I believe, in a personal way as this stillness continued throughout meditation."

This meditative moment also appears to have a resonance

Chapter Seven: The Formative Presence of Children

within her as well.

The importance of the meditative moments with children in terms of nourishing the adult is also evident in the following two excerpts by Domenica. She records two different times when the children are gathered to meditate together on the True Vine parable. Because of the significance they have for her, both of these accounts, written one week apart, are included. ("Child" indicates the responses of different children; "C" represents the catechist.) One senses an eagerness in Domenica to capture the flow of this meditation, as seen in the following incomplete phrases and sentences. She titles it: "Meditation—The True Vine—Communion Group."

[C]:	Things to look at while meditating. Who does the candle remind us of?
[Child]:	Jesus.
	The Great Light.
[C]:	What does the Shepherd [do] for his sheep?
[Child]:	He takes care of his sheep if has 100 sheep.
	—one gets lost He searches—rejoices.
[C]:	Why?
[Child]:	He loves them.
[C]:	How do the sheep feel?
[Child]:	—good and happy.
[C]:	Who are his sheep?
[Child]:	—Us.

Like Leaven

[C]: Jesus said, "I am the True Vine. You are the branches."
What does sap do for [your branch]?

[Child]: Gives it food.
Helps it live.

[C]: Whose life could be flowing in the sap?

[Child]: Ours.

[C]: Where does it come from?

[Child]: God.
Jesus would give up his life for ours.
Jesus rose again.
He ascended into heaven.

[C]: How long does Jesus' life last now?

[Child]: Forever.

[C]: I wonder when your bud would appear on the True Vine.

[Child]: Baptism.
In your mother's stomach.
When you were born.

[C]: What happens?

[Child]: You open and flower and grow.

[C]: What came inside the branch?

[Child]: Sap.

[C]: Are all the branches the same?

Chapter Seven: The Formative Presence of Children

[Child]: No.

[C]: What could we do to let more sap come to your branch?

[Child]: Pray.
Try to follow the commandments.
Help each other.
To forgive.
Do extra things to help.
To meditate.
My mom meditates each morning.
To sing.

[C]: How green would it be?

[Child]: As green as a plant could get.

[C]: Vine and branches—how are they?

[Child]: Already attached.
Have to stay at a good level of sap.

[C]: What does Jesus ask us to do?

[Child]: To remain.

The following week in the atrium, the children reflect again on the True Vine parable:

[C]: Jesus said, "Who am I?"…do you remember?

[Child]: I am the Good Shepherd. I am the True Vine.

[C]: Who [is] the vinedresser? Who takes care of the plant?

Like Leaven

[Child]: God.

[C]: "True" - what do you think this means?

[Child]: Real. Possible.

[C]: If something is true, would it change?

[Child]: No.

[C]: What happens when sap flows through the vine?

[Child]: It grows.
Many leaves.
Energy.

[C]: What would branch be like if blocked, had no sap?

[Child]: Unhealthy.
And sick.
Leaves might all fall off.

[C]: What do you think [would happen to the branch] when a person dies?

[Child]: Branch will still be there.
Branch receives new life.

Chapter Seven: The Formative Presence of Children

Part Two: The Atrium: Environment of Encounter

We recall that when speaking about these moments of celebration—listening to God, and meditating with children—that they are happening in an atrium environment. The atrium has a very important role in facilitating encounters at many levels. For instance, there is the child's encounter with God, the child's encounter with other children and with the adult, as well as the adult's encounter with God and with children.

In fact, the atrium is a factor that significantly affects the adult's relationship with children. Obviously, it is more than just a room. Rather, it serves to provide an atmosphere which facilitates the relationship with God in a particular way. Here we will touch on only two of the facets of the atrium from the adults' perspective. The first, as a place of encounter with children. The second, as a place for the adult's encounter with God.

Place of Encounter with Children

The first facet concerns the fact that the atrium is a specifically prepared place. As such, it is especially conducive for the child's own activity, independent of the adult. Thus it affords the adult the opportunity to observe the child's quality of interaction with the Christian message and the materials that incarnate it, so to speak.[90] For example, Wendy observes: "All children today engaged in work that seemed practical and highly tactile." She adds her image for the atrium, "our vineyard that is the atrium," thereby indicating the atrium as a place of growth and fruitfulness.

Recall that these journal reflections were written during the specific time of retreat in preparation for the sacraments of Reconciliation and Eucharist. Thus there are frequent allusions to the way in which the atrium has been arranged in an even more special way in the light of this retreat experience. As Domenica describes: "The atrium was inviting—dimly lighted, soft music, perfume from beautiful flowers." She notes that the children enter with pleasure: "[their] surprise in the environment which has changed—noticed and smelled the white carnations—noticed the new white placemats" all of which "were pointed out [to her] by the children."

The retreat atmosphere serves as a welcoming invitation to the child's activity, as Eileen notes in this excerpt:

> "excitement in 'body' and 'talk', such smiles, room that was dimmed with music seemed 'quieter' than other room (even though music heard), children anxious to do own work."

Kate also remarked on the effect the retreat atmosphere has on the children: "They were quiet, in awe of the surroundings—we had decorated with a lot of plants, we're only using candle light." In another journal reflection during the retreat time, Kate mentioned specifically the area of the atrium arranged as a "prayer corner." Here she describes the children's reactions in discovering this area of the atrium. She adds her own question to herself as well:

> "They all discovered the prayer corner and four of the children were actually standing in a line waiting to get a turn; how is it that this communication among the children happens so quickly?"

Chapter Seven: The Formative Presence of Children

Place for the Adult's Encounter with God

These excerpts speak about the atrium as a place that provides, in the physical sense of the word, opportunities for the child's activity or "work." It is also a space prepared to assist the child's meditation and prayer. And it calls forth prayer not only in the children but in the adults as well. Wendy writes:

> "It is important for all of us in the Atrium to allow God's stillness and silence to breathe within us, so it can circulate freely, and be among us, thus being with Him, who has died and risen for us."

These two other brief excerpts by Wendy indicate that the atrium offers the adult opportunities to meet God. She writes on two separate occasions:

> "I felt the Holiness of God fill our Atrium."

> "In moments of humility and stillness in the Atrium, I have come to understand that many wonderful things can happen to us, as Christ gives us so much."

That the atrium is actually a formative place for the adult as well as the children is true not only for a relative newcomer like Wendy. It also holds true for someone who has worked over ten years' in an atrium, such as Eileen. Here she reflects on the experience of being in the atrium with the children during the time of their retreat. She mentions the impact of this experience on her too:

> "—I love to share this joy and excitement.
> —The need exists: to focus this joy and excitement; not subdue it.
> —The need for quiet and order is important to this focus but it must be gentle and natural.

They are truly happy to be at this point in their journey."

Part 3: Gifts from Children

The Theme of Gift

The catechists' reflections about children are rich in terms of what they are given to observe, to understand, to experience, and even to be challenged about. Essentially, what they are speaking about can be identified in terms of gifts.

This opening reflection by Eileen names it as such—"gift." She indicates that being with children assumes the nature of the gift in three ways. First, it is simply to be there with children and to see their quality of responsiveness. Second, this quality in turn draws her more deeply into appreciating and experiencing the power of the parable. Third, it is to see the children's capacity for surrender in the relationship with God, and how this is an invitation in terms of her attitudes towards them.

> "This time with the children was one of gift.
> I had a sense that the children and the adults present were receiving each word that Jesus was giving to us, to each one of us.
> The complete attention; facial, physical, conversational, spoke to me in such a way that it became even clearer to me why our Lord chose this Parable [True Vine]. It seemed to be constantly opening before me and yet enclosing each of us within. The peace remained with us as we began individual work.
> We must respect and be in awe of the full attention and such quiet in people we view as rambunctious

and fully sociable! It is their need; their giving over!"

Faith, Hope, and Love

Our exploration touches on the theological gifts of faith, hope and love. Yet, naming these "gifts" also includes what may be seen as the provocative or challenging aspects they may contain.

This is indicated in the following reflection by Kate, which she titles "the True Vine." It opens with a recognition of "the wavering gift of faith." Then she probes this "precious gift of faith" in terms of her role of proclaiming the "good news" to children. As she ponders, she affirms that children "possess the gift of faith." That the children are "gifted with faith" spurs her to prayer, specifically for "more faith." In this account, Kate's desire for more faith is directly connected with experiencing the child's gift of faith:

> "—How <u>wonderful</u> is the good news—that to be fruitful we need only REMAIN in the vine; that God tends to me and ensures that I have the sap, the life of the Risen Christ running through my veins…what more could I want or ask?
>
> —It is that wavering gift of faith however that sometimes isn't strong enough to appreciate the joy and love to be found in this good news revealed to us by Jesus.
>
> —The revelation, the words don't make any sense unless I possess that precious gift of faith.
>
> So what does this say about evangelization? About proclaiming?

It seems to me it would be impossible to proclaim the good news to anyone who doesn't have the gift of faith.

—With the children (possibly with everyone) we need to proclaim the good news in its entirety, in its abundance, in its fullness assuming that the children possess the gift of faith and you know I think children do have this gift.

Look at how they respond to our proclamations!! Is it simply because we are adults and somehow authority figures? Is it because they are a 'blank slate' and can have anything written on them?

Or are they gifted with faith and thus with a <u>need</u> for a relationship with God, and an acceptance in joy of the truth of the good news? We need to assume they are faith-filled, I think, or we could harm the potential of their relationship. And I need to pray for <u>more</u> faith so I can respond or present in truth to their needs and potential <u>and</u> because I'm sure my life could be more FILLED, had I more faith."

Ruth is struck by a similar awareness of what the children have to give. In her case, the gift is linked to hope: "I'm hopeful knowing that in our work with the children, in their natural state of being, we have the opportunity of learning so much."

As to the gift of love, Domenica records this incident:

"One child spent 15 minutes in the prayer room meditating while all others were working fervently on booklets. She was so calm on the kneeler, meditating on a picture above."

Chapter Seven: The Formative Presence of Children

Then, on another journal page, she returns to that incident, naming for herself what attracted her to that moment, which still lingered within her:

> "I felt jealous almost of the child serenely meditating in the prayer room. She seemed so peaceful, I guess I felt the need for peace as well. She seemed so intense with her feelings. She also knew when it was time to leave the prayer room. So focused on the love and peace of Jesus."

Joy

In an overall sense, joy is prevalent in all the catechists' writing about their time with children. On the one hand, simply being with children seems to bring joy. Wendy writes: "The children have changed profoundly over the last three years. I am so glad I was there with them." On the other hand, it can be a specific moment. Kate records a moment of joy that seems to surprise her. She explains that she overheard a discussion the children were having as they chose colored markers. The fact that she had recorded it so carefully suggests that she in turn was delighted by their joy. She writes:

> "This is so much fun," M.J. [child].
>
> "You call this fun?" E. [child].
>
> I believe she meant this time was very special, but fun wasn't the right word to describe it because her father told us the next morning that she hadn't slept all night, so anxious was she to get back to the atrium.
>
> [child] – energetic but not an enthusiastic boy agreed that it was fun. These three children are missing their 'Fun Day' at the school on Friday and this is the first

I've heard about it, so I presume no one minded too much."

Wonder

Francesca records the experience of the closing Eucharistic liturgy for the children's group as a "beautiful time" for her. It is principally the way the children relate to God that gives something to her personally. For her, seeing children in this way is tantamount to being aware of the coming and the presence of the Kingdom of God:

> "Before we stop our regular sessions for the year, we end with a mass for 6-9 year olds. It's a very beautiful time that is prepared by the children the week before. One of the most animated and verbal moments is when they get to pick the readings for the mass. Even before we do this I know that one of the requests to be read will be the True Vine.
>
> [They say:] 'Yes', first the True Vine and then other suggestions come. And so the response of the child 6-9 years old is not just immediate and kept within the retreat. The hunger is before, during, and I dare say in their relationship with the Good Shepherd, their response is so deep it has an eternal quality—now how can you measure that but in the coming of the Kingdom."

This note of wonder can be detected in the following observation by Kate as well; it also reveals what is challenging for her. She is caught by the unpredictability of children, and the manner in which they put to the test one's own interpretations of their actions. This comes as a "surprise" to her:

Chapter Seven: The Formative Presence of Children

"—Sometimes the body language of children can be deceiving. I think the children can't possibly be listening and then they surprise me. J. [child] was a prime example. She cannot sit still on a chair when we are gathered in a group; she can easily frustrate me when I'm presenting. Often I will try to ignore her disruptiveness because stopping and waiting for her wouldn't allow us to even finish a presentation. Later she might say something which reveals she heard the presentation and in fact has been meditating on it—AMAZING."

Prayer

Children's capacity for prayer is very striking to the catechists. Even to "witness" the child's way of praying appears to be a privilege, as seen in the following excerpts by Wendy. It can be the experience of simply watching one child at the miniature altar table in the atrium:

"Again I am witnessing prayer. Today, J. [child] prepared the altar. The moment arrived when everything was placed as she wanted it to be. She opened the missal, made the sign of the cross, bowed her head, and prayed, hands joined together. She appeared both solemn and joyful, very much with God."

Or it can be observing the group of children as a whole that once again prompts this sense of being a privileged witness. Wendy makes explicit that this experience is also an invitation to pray:

"I witness our atrium becoming a community. We cross over the time and space, our different ages and backgrounds, together we love and praise God. In song and discussion we are joined and transformed into praise, moving in and out of the moments of prayer and wonder."

In this final excerpt from Wendy, we get the overall sense of this experience for her. It spreads beyond the boundaries of the atrium:

"The catechesis continues to inspire me in very creative and what I would term, soulful ways. This is especially true after I have been with the children [...]. Often after my sessions with the children I will go home and listen to very soft music."

A Way of Being

This excerpt is from Eileen. It is her reflection on a message contained in the True Vine parable on "being" and "doing." She highlights an important element that runs through the reflections of all the catechists as a gift given to them by children. That is, the invitation to a different way of "being" as adults:

" 'BEING': focus being placed on the fact that 'being' is very difficult in comparison to 'doing.' But that 'being' (remaining) brings 'doing' (fruit). Children very naturally, very effortlessly enjoy and continue to Remain. As adults, we 'do' to legitimize ourselves, <u>value ourselves</u>, desire others to <u>value us</u>, all by doing. Is this the fruit that glorifies the Father? To say that we need to learn this quality of being is saying that we receive a great gift from the children when we experience it."

Domenica offered this reflection at the end of our time together. It is offered here as an image that suggests an inclusive "cycle"

Chapter Seven: The Formative Presence of Children

of relationships. As well, it serves as a fitting conclusion to this chapter because it speaks so clearly of the child's formative presence (also synthesized in the graph below):

> "It's a kind of cycle. It reinforces us when we see that spark [in the children], or when we see that drive; it brings us closer and then we do something better. It's just a cycle. You touch me, I touch you, and we're touching God together."

Figure 2

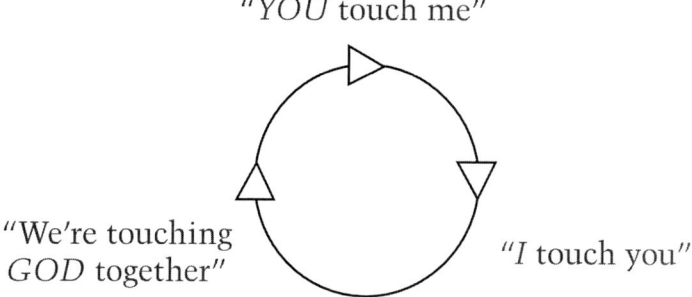

Chapter Eight:
Dynamics of Relationship

This chapter attends to the dynamics at the heart of the formation process. The aspect that appears to underlie them all is relationship.

We look at three movements linked to relationship that emerged from the catechists' experience: a) communion, community and mission; b) conversion; and c) the multi-levelled experience of the formation process itself. Or, to use a metaphor, the catechists' experience of the course and atrium components are like musical compositions in which these three movements are heard:

Within the catechist there seems to be a movement towards communion with God, to community with others, and to mission (particularly this catechesis with children).

Within the call to be a catechist, there is another movement that appears as a call to conversion.

Within the course experience there is a movement of levels: information, formation, towards transformation.

Some of these aspects will be revisited in detail in following chapters. Only a few examples from the catechists' journals about each of these movements/dynamics are presented here.

Chapter Eight: Dynamics of Relationship

Part 1: Communion, Community, Mission

The first dynamic discernible in the formation process, understood as inclusive of both the course and the atrium experience, is the following movement from

- communion with God, and thus oneself as well;
- to community with the other adults in the catechesis, and children;
- into mission and ministry, in this case with children.[91]

There is a constant interplay among these three movements, since all aspects of the catechists' experience are included. Thus it is not possible to separate them in a clearly demarked way; however, at least they will be highlighted here.

Communion

Francesca is reflecting on the True Vine parable, and expresses the invitation she hears in it: to "remain". In descriptive language, she imagines a scenario that spans a lifetime. It begins as "a two-year old,", onto "a teenager now about to grow up," and into future time as "an old lady":

> "Yeah, I know there is someone who loves me, now, today, tomorrow and it's God. I'm really grateful....I really heard the word REMAIN. I want to run, I want to be free. I want to 'do it by myself'. I'm like a 2-year old. I want to be independent and do it by myself. [...] I feel like a teenager now about to grow up. I remain because I resign myself to my mortality and all my mediocre abilities. I'll go along for the ride. I'll wait, remain and stay. [...] Now I feel like an old lady, a

little fragile, broken and resigned to this life. It's not so bad counting on God to produce the sap and tend the vines. I like the attention, the care. O.K. so we all make up a team. This life is a team effort, I guess. Ya, OK, I'll remain, I'm in good company."

Domenica reflects on her relationship with God in her course journal:

"We are reminded that God, our Father, continually loves us and holds us in high esteem. Perhaps if more people felt their importance to God, they would act differently. I know I need to be reminded often so that I can grow and change to become a better person, a person of service, but with dignity. Too many people feel downtrodden by society. And the response is not a positive one."[92]

From her relationship with God, she moves to her ministry with children:

"I find I, as an adult, need time, much time to internalize and really feel the revelation happening. As an educator, I know that some children need more time than others to internalize, so coming back to the parable after a period of time could be more fruitful and the children will be ready to receive more information or enjoy more and more the revelation of the Good News."

These closing words of Domenica's reflection also show the interrelationship between one's own faith life and apostolic life.

Wendy is attending to what "is happening in [her] soul":

"However in our human form, we may not always be fully able to understand what is happening within our souls, where the curtains are drawn, and shadows of day to day living hide inner reflection (especially for someone like me, who always feels that I am running against the clock to get things done)."

This insight seems to germinate within her across time. During a later period of reflection, she writes, "I feel within me the building of my ministry, my work to do in God's name, and my love for all of this deepen." Later still, she recalls the experience of being in the atrium with children: "Sometimes after leaving the Atrium… I think about the children at the Atrium. I want this world we live in to be a better place, especially for them." Wendy moves from that moment of being present to God and herself into her sense of mission, lived in "in God's name."

Community

Various aspects in the catechists' course journals indicate the movement towards community. This dimension of community will be examined in the following chapters, as we said. Here we identify briefly four different aspects of community articulated by the catechists.

The first and most common aspect was an appreciation of the opportunity for dialogue, because it so enriches and enlivens experience. To use Francesca's words: "I enjoyed the adult moments of discussion. It helps to reshape it and keep it alive." Discussion can also evoke deep personal reflection. For example, Kate's following reflection about "transformation" was evoked by a discussion on the theme of the history of the kingdom of God.

> "…the way in which we have transformed our environment is truly phenomenal and our

transformations are continually progressing, developing and growing. Each invention or transformation is usually built on the ones preceeding it. In other words, I don't think I personally could use natural elements to produce fire and yet I use fire all the time to transform other things. The people inventing computer chips might not be able to create a simple motor out of the natural environment and yet the environment that they grew up in provides them with the resources to go even further into the unknown. We creatures truly are fascinating.

And why did God do this?

Why were we made this way?"

A second aspect of community relates to the collaborative presence of others. Ruth writes: "I really appreciate to hear other people's ideas—stretches my brain—and excites me." Ruth also notes that there is a particular quality to this collaboration: "I have no particular comment, except [I] always appreciate the graciousness and commitment of Francesca. Graciousness in welcoming us, and obvious commitment in her work and sharing her experience."

Domenica is struck by the quality of mutual presence among the catechists, and the faith with which they approach the biblical message in the course context. In three different excerpts she underscored the importance of community. She also identified significant aspects in this communal experience. One is linked to Ruth's impression, just stated: "Perhaps the respect and high regard that is given to those who are ready to receive the message is what attracts me to this course." Another is the shared commitment to faith and ministry. This generates a bond between Domenica and others

Chapter Eight: Dynamics of Relationship

in the formation experience: "I loved the participation in the Synthesis of the Mass and the closeness we all feel to each other as we experience the Monday night [course] moments together." Finally, this bond supersedes what could be termed simply a learning experience among co-learners. It deepens into what Domenica indicates as an atmosphere of shared prayer:

> "This made me reflect on the wonderful feeling, the focusing and wonderful prayerfulness of our group. This is the way we should always feel during Mass— our hearts should feel so full of honest love for God and closeness to each other. Is this not what the Good Shepherd wishes for all of us, all the time? During our class, there is such a tone of respect for each other along with a <u>yearning</u> to hear, learn and understand more and more. Can I say—happy expectation. Yes, this is what I feel."

A third aspect of community is illustrated by Eileen's reflection, in which community is seen as challenge as well as gift. A course discussion elicits what Eileen calls thoughts of a "practical" nature:

> "A practical reflection came to me as well. We each have different experiences with the children we are involved with. This shapes our 'sharing' with other catechists. Indeed our way with children, people in general, is very individual and I suppose we must embrace this reality."

She also notes the contribution of personal differences among the catechists: "In particular ways individual differences can be very 'effective'."

A fourth aspect of community is addressed in an over-arching way in the following excerpt by Wendy. She speaks of the significance of the gifts of others in community, especially as called together and sustained by the Holy Spirit:

> "We all bring our own hearts and we place them on the table. As at a party, we offer gifts. No gift is greater than the next, they are all the same. We are unified in the spirit of our sharing, like the Holy Spirit—he gives us these gifts, and no one is greater than the other. They are all the same, all great. These gifts, they come in all shapes and sizes, but all are great. I imagine all of us [catechists] sometimes as we sit around the table… We wait for each other's words; we listen for them, we hear each other, in words and silence. Calmness, with a current running through, seems to be the approach of this work."

Mission

The above aspects manifest the importance of community, both in facilitating communion with God and with oneself, and also in its influence on one's ministry. As we said, the influence community has on one's personal growth and service to children are addressed explicitly in the next chapter. Therefore, only this excerpt will be offered now by way of illustrating the call to mission. It is a reflection by Wendy, which she titled, "Reflections on the Call of the Catechesis":

> "When one works with the children in this way, one understands and sees very early on that it is different from any other working of religious education; without 'knowing' all of the presentations, as of course when one begins one cannot possibly know. There is a certain

gentleness with which my commitment to this work has been built. In so many other types of work, there are comparisons drawn, between people, institutions... there are leaders and mentors even. The Catechesis of the Good Shepherd has been and continues to be an affirming human restorative for me. There is no competition, no judgment...."

The following chart represents a summary of these three movements mentioned above: a) communion with God and self; b) community with children and other catechists; and c) the movement into the mission. Before concluding, we note that the document entitled *The Church in America* presents insights into these movements, under the headings: encounter/communion, conversion, community, and ministry/mission.[93]

Three Movements:
Communion, Community, and Mission

Communion with God and oneself	Community with Catechists	Community with Children—Atrium	Mission with Children	Mission with Children
(Communion) →→	(Community) →→	(Community) →→	(Mission) →→	(Mission) →→
Communion	Dialogue	Wendy Francesca	Catechist-in-ministry: Call: as a catechist	Catechist-in-formation: "Course" process: Information
Community	Collaboration Shared Faith	Eileen Domenica	Call within a call: to conversion	Formation
Mission	Shared Ministry	Mary Kate Ruth		Transformation

Chapter Eight: Dynamics of Relationship

Part 2: A Call Within a Call

We have already noted the aspect of vocation at work in the lives of these catechists. When looking at their accounts with a wide-angle lens to see what they reveal about the catechists' journey as a whole, a second movement is discerned. That is, there seems to be a call within a call. Within their shared call to catechesis with children, there is another call, personal to each individual, represented in the movement towards what may be named conversion.

When we addressed the sense of call that each of these seven catechists experienced with respect to the catechesis (Chapter Two), we also spoke about the challenges they encountered, which already indicated some of the costs in responding to this call. In some way such costs imply conversion. As Kate says: "So much is asked of the catechist."

Additionally, there is also a sense that this original call opens onto a horizon which draws forth from the catechists a willingness, or in some cases even a desire, to enter more deeply into the growth and change that the call embodies. It appears as a movement toward interiority, which then moves towards choice, action, and so forth. This is illustrated in the continuation of Kate's excerpt above: "So much is asked of the catechist in this catechesis but at the same time it is a gift. The inspiration to reflect further, <u>the need to reflect further causes me to reflect further!!</u>" (her emphasis).

Francesca's journal relating to the children's retreat contains echoes of this. The cost of commitment is evident. So too is the openness to surrender, and the glimmers of expectancy that this brings new life or, in her words, contains a "promise":

"First Communion Retreat completed. We're 'done'... I did all I could do. I'm happy about that. I really get lost in the work. It becomes so focused, so single-hearted. I lost myself in this retreat. It was like total surrender. The promise is I will find myself. I hope so."

Conversion here is seen in its literal meaning: turning toward. Perhaps it is also a turning toward another, and more explicitly, turning toward God, the one who fulfills the promise.

This openness to conversion appears to contain within it an invitation that involves both a letting go and a letting come.[94] In Wendy's words: "I am learning to let go of the desire to know and understand. I am discovering my desire to experience mystery. As much as he [Christ] has given us, I find it exciting to know that there will be more."

This call to an interior change or conversion is received by Ruth not only as a catechist, but also on the level of her personal life: "Also more challenged in my own life to 'stretch' and also as a catechist to live with the 'Word'; then I come to the reality that I am a 'doer' by nature, and would love to 'just be'."

The concern with "doing" versus "being" is not particular to Ruth alone. It is present in many catechists' reflections on the manner in which the catechesis calls them forth to a different way of being. And it is expressed with different colorations. For Eileen, it is the call to trust: "I realize it is all a matter of trust. We must step back and trust the children to make, create, celebrate. I have seen the wonderful results when we relinquish the role of director and become facilitator. Dignity is communicated though unspoken." Further, this relinquishment of a certain kind of attitude vis-à-vis the child is for the sake of a higher purpose: "We must trust the child and the Holy Spirit working within the child. We must allow time and space for

Chapter Eight: Dynamics of Relationship

this relationship; it is why we are there."

In a similar vein, this invitation to empower children by a greater giving over of freedom to them is manifest in the reflection of Mary at the completion of the retreat: "After just finishing our retreat—the comments on retreat made a clear impact. We were not free enough in letting the children plan celebrations during our retreat… I could see how we had not entered into that whole process… However, next year I think it will be different."

Conversion is a continuous process. It has a future dimension to it, in which the Holy Spirit is at work. Kate illustrates this in describing a moment during the retreat when she and five children had gathered together to go over the readings for one of the celebrations:

> "They [children] wanted to keep reading over and over and over because they wanted to be able to say it well (proclaim it). I was very impressed with their desire and willingness to work at it without a suggestion from me. It says so much about knowing when to let go, knowing when to trust the children and trusting the Spirit. After all, it's God's work, not mine. (And God will love me just as much even if it 'flops' (according to me); but will I be able to love myself as much??)."

Finally it appears that embarking on an ongoing formation process offers an opportunity to hear and to catch hold of the stirring within oneself of a call to deeper growth. Listening to the True Vine parable, the word "remain" lingers within Domenica: "To experience the joy of relationship with God and others we must feel the peace (Christ's peace) in our hearts, knowing, really knowing that it's where it's meant to be. Remain." There is an invitation heard in these words, which Domenica expresses this way:

> "I'm wondering what kind of an effort am I really making to go to Mass more often than once or twice a week. After most of our classes, I feel a great anticipation to be closer to God. Perhaps it's the words, the inspirations, the meditations, or a combination but I want to feel more joy in being in relationship with God. I want to become a little more perfect or strive to achieve closer to the goal of being perfect for me—being a little bit of a better person."

Part 3: Learning Process:
Information, Formation, Transformation

This reference to "our classes"—the formation course—in Domenica's reflection points to the third movement we mentioned. The catechists' journals provided glimpses of a multi-leveled experience, one which has an aperture toward hidden regions within the individuals themselves.

This third movement as it relates to the course experience is from an informational level to a formational level, with indications of its transformational potential. That is to say, from the catechists' reflections on the course, it could be seen as a process that moves from information, to formation, and possibly into transformation. There is a deepening movement occurring even during the short time that the catechists recorded their reflections (eight weeks). Certainly it relates to the informational aspect of the formation course, but also and more importantly, to the formational level in the real sense of that word, and at times even the level of transformation.

To illustrate the manner in which this trifold dimension—

Chapter Eight: Dynamics of Relationship

information, formation, and transformation—is present within the course experience, only a few of the catechists' reflections will be selected. This will be done with little commentary because this dimension will be looked at again in more detail in the next chapters.

For Ruth the course is obviously informative: "The thought that remains in my mind is the impressionistic idea that 'engaging the imagination' we stimulate religious sense of awe." And, naturally, there is an expectation that it be informative: "I had a sense of relief that the possibility was there to present it [the material] in 3 moments." Ruth was also delighted about the handouts relating to the children's retreats: "The package on 'Retreats'. It looks great. I'm almost sad that we have to wait one year before we are involved in another Retreat."[95] However, there is the insistence that this be more than an informative experience: "I'm again frustrated by the speed of things being presented, as I need more time to feel the moment."

"Feeling the moment" is an indicator of the need for time to interiorize what is being lived: "I felt more relaxed after tonight's presentation and class. Not as rushed and I don't feel like I missed anything and have to go home and piece it together." While Ruth has a need for practical training, she also needs space and time to incorporate what is given. "Since the True Vine was first presented," she notes in her reflection, "I've been very anxious to get every word, as I had to present it to the First Communion children on several occasions. Now that the retreat is finished, this is the first night I can enter into the moment…." The reason for, and the significance of, "entering into the moment" is reiterated in another of her reflections: "The first time I heard the presentation of the Good Shepherd, I was in great awe—and recall the feeling frequently when preparing for presentations or reliving the moment of love that

Jesus has for us." Perhaps the phrase "reliving the moment of love that Jesus has for us" contain hints that something transforming is taking place?

A similar movement can be gleaned from Mary's journal. She speaks about qualities that open her to the transcendent: "The beauty and truth of the presentation of the material never fails to make me happy." She writes elsewhere: "The significance of a few words, of what is said and in what order—the profoundness of this—that the small can be so great—the subtle so powerful, this touched me tonight." Again, she refers to the presentation of the True Vine parable in terms of a light for her path in future ministry: "The sequence, or outline, of the True Vine helped to put that long flow into focus—to give emphasis to each side of the mystery in turn. There is always so much more—I feel so rich after each of these classes—the way is being lighted."

In this final excerpt, Mary intimates a growing experience, specifically in relation to the gestures of offering, the breaking of bread, and the exchange of peace in the Eucharist: "The gift that comes down; is given back up; and then the gift that spreads. I thought I knew <u>enough</u> about the Mass but it is becoming so much more" (her emphasis).

For Wendy the course is clearly more than an "academic" experience: "In the atrium, and here [University of St. Michael's College], we find that the theme is always the same. There is a way to be simple and clear. There is a way to 'be' and peace, as we are transferring/sharing God's love (message and meaning, Jesus) to the children and each other, with our hands, our ears, our voice." The same strain of that being/doing melody can be heard here. In this second reflection, Wendy uses an image to symbolize the formation-transformation

Chapter Eight: Dynamics of Relationship

movement happening: "The Catechesis is an open door, always saying welcome to those who enter; shalom, peace. You have a place here. I hear this always when I sit with other catechists; the voice of love and welcoming, as we look beyond what is seen and search for what is unseen, to the greater life."

Domenica appreciates qualities in the formation course that are not typically associated solely with a "learning" experience. Three excerpts, each a sentence long, are sufficient to indicate this course experience as potentially transformative:

> "This course and class inspire me to get closer to our Father so that I may feel the peace and joy of Christ in me."

> "This time in the course gives me time to meditate and gives me new avenues via the catechesis to experience God's undying love for us."

> "Listening to these seminars helps me to love as Jesus loves—'to be'
> —this is the attraction
> —this is the reception
> —inspiration happens at these seminars."

In closing this chapter, two excerpts by Kate will be offered. The first is from her course journal, where she is reflecting in a generic way on the "message and the materials" presented. It contains the recognition of what this catechesis asks of the catechist. Then it moves to another dimension, towards transformation, as is suggested by her final words: "Prayer…"

> "It feels like <u>so</u> much preparation is required in order to pass these wonderful treasures on to the children in the right way. Certainly it can't be that the message, or the truth is vulnerable, yet it seems that we could

damage the message, or damage the child's perception or understanding of it, if we are not fully prepared. And how to be fully prepared?? Besides, of course all the knowledge that is impacted through the classes and written materials, we need to internalize the message. That can only happen through our own prayer, study and reflection."

The second excerpt is taken from Kate's comments during our final group reflection day in the following January. Looking back across many months, Kate offers a summary of the course experience (the April-June semester). She also identifies a key factor in the process: the dynamic of attentiveness. Certainly there is an invitation not only to "learn," both in the course and the atrium, but also to reflect on these experiences as well:

"When I think of a course, I think of something fairly academic—you go and you 'learn.' That journaling made such a difference. In fact, the work that we're doing is not just something 'academic.' It's much more than that. It involves our spirituality and who we are, and what we offer the children. In a sense it is a very important element…. The journaling does allow us to attend to our own personal spirituality and our deeper self. It's not just 'learning'—this is what you do and how you do it, this is the theory behind it, and this is the way it works. But it involves us very personally and that is very important. It's so much more than just an 'academic' course."

This excerpt highlights the importance of the reflection and observation activities for the catechists, both in terms of their theoretical learning (course), as well as the experiential learning (atrium). Since these attentiveness exercises seemed

Chapter Eight: Dynamics of Relationship

to represent a major contribution for the catechists, they will be further treated in the next chapter, particularly in terms of their formative possibilities.

Chapter Nine:
Ways of Accompaniment

"Listen to me; pay attention" (Isaiah 49:1)

Three months after completing the course and atrium components of our research process, we gathered as a small group for a day of reflection (September). Brother Ignatius Feaver served as our facilitator. He opened our time together by inviting the catechists to reflect on their experience:

> "I invite you now to reflect on this time period of the last few months since you finished your journal. What has been your experience: new awareness, joys, frustrations, surprises?"

Each catechist responded in the form of a personal story. Their responses revolved around two basic points.

The first point related to the experience of the course. They singled out the reflection practice. That is, the fifteen minutes at the end of each course session they dedicated to writing in their journals. The second point related to their ministry experience with children. They focused on the activity of writing their observations of children, and their reflections on their atrium experience (outlined in Chapter 1).

Overall, their personal stories represented an afterword to the three-month course and atrium phase. That is, they contain a reflection on their reflections (during the course), and an observation about their observations of the children (in the atrium).

Chapter Nine: Ways of Accompaniment

Listening at a later date to the tape recordings of their stories gave the impression of hearing variations on a musical theme. In summarizing their experience with respect to these two orbits—course and atrium—emphasis was given to the attentiveness exercises they worked on during this time. The term attentiveness is used to encompass both activities of reflection and observation. For a seminal study on the spiritual significance of the faculty of attention, see Simone Weil's "Reflections on the Right Use of School Studies with a View to the Love of God."[96]

In the first part of this chapter, their course experience will be treated by drawing on the catechists' words. Then some implications will be examined, especially with regard to the underlying thematic of reflection itself. In the second part of this chapter, their ministry experience will be treated by drawing on the catechists' accounts once again. Each excerpt will be looked at in terms of key implications it contains, particularly with regard to the practice of observation.

Part 1: Reflection

Eileen:
"It goes through to my formation with the children."

Eileen has been in the catechesis 11 years and is a busy mother of four children. We recall her earlier reflections in which she emphasized the child's need to receive the biblical-liturgical themes in a measured manner. And, using the image of water falling on the ground, she stressed the child's need for adequate time to absorb the Christian message. In the following excerpt, Eileen conveys the importance of the *adult's* need for time to be receptive to the Word.

"When we did take that few minutes after the lecture, after our time as adults together, I found that very valuable. Because I find that I'm 'there,' and then I'm gone out of there. I think it's really permeated, and it's gone in. I really did value those reflection times… I think it really was a good exercise, that I never would do myself. It's very little time, but…there usually was one particular thing that I would hang on to. It might not have been something that the group hung on to at all. Obviously, as an adult, it benefits me, but it goes through to my formation then with the children. That was to me valuable. I enjoyed that."

Here Eileen seems to echo her earlier words about the child's needs. Now, however, Eileen is speaking of that as a personal need too. That is, the image she had formerly applied to the child—the plant's need to be able to absorb the water—now appears to apply to herself too: "it's really permeated." One thinks of the biblical image of the seed (Isaiah 55:10-11), which requires a receptive soil and time for the seed to take root and fructify.

Francesca:
"It was that moment of falling in love again."

Francesca, 10 years in the catechesis, appreciates the opportunity to dwell on the theological themes, especially creation, which have helped her to reflect on her relationship with God. We recall her earlier reference to the conviction that presenting the Christian message to children is like planting seeds, which she believes will grow inside them over time. This appears no less true for adults as well, because we see here that she experienced a germination time, which became fruitful in the gift of prayer.

Chapter Nine: Ways of Accompaniment

"I think for me too, I've taken the course before.... So I allowed myself to go into it in another way, in a deeper way, but more than just doing it to take it back to the six to nine-year olds [children], but doing it for me. So it was more of a personal journey.... I enjoyed taking the fifteen minutes afterwards and writing down some things because what would happen was, in the class, I would be struck by something...a line, or a few words and it hit me where I was in my life, and I would be gone! It was like every time you came down [to the seminar] you knew you were going to get a gift.... You couldn't predict it, you couldn't plan it and you couldn't set it up. [For example] something about creation, and it would just be exactly what I needed to hear for that time, and I would put a little star beside it. Then, sometime the next day, I would write out pages or I'd think about it, and I found that to be good.

That was very much like hearing about the catechesis for the first time. It was that moment of falling in love again, just hearing about it again; it was hearing some new things, and the same things just going deeper, and that was very comforting.

I didn't hand in my journal on time...I allowed myself the time over the summer to go back over those notes and what was in my mind, because tending to keep things in your head is very hard, and it's freeing again when you put it down on paper. I'm starting to develop a prayer.... The prayer became really a way to get through things."

Francesca's accounts indicate she has been touched on the level of her own identity by means of prolonged reflection. Taken as a whole, her comments suggest these words by Thomas Merton: "To put it better, we are even called to share with God the work of creating the truth of our identity.... It demands close attention to reality at every moment, and great fidelity to God.... The seeds that are planted in my liberty at every moment, by God's will, are the seeds of my own identity, my own reality...."[97]

Kate:
"I think it's a very important part of me."

Kate is also a busy mother of four children, and she has nine years of very active involvement in the atrium. Here the accent is on the need for the time and means for reflection and meditation.

> "I found the time after the lecture as well to be very, very fruitful. It allowed me to in some way be a bit meditative, reflective, something that I often yearn to do, but am not very good at making the time to do. Having that chunk [of time] there really helped that. I think it's a very important part for me, partly because this is the kind of thing that in a sense we are encouraging the children to enter into, and to be meditative and contemplative in the atrium. If I can't do that myself, it's pretty hard to imagine that I could be able to create an atmosphere that would encourage that in the children."

Kate's desire to become more reflective indicates a vital point. If we are to be able to accompany children on their spiritual journey we need to be nurtured ourselves, especially in terms of allowing ourselves the time to stop and reflect. Her reflection brings to mind this passage in Anne Morrow Lindbergh's

Chapter Nine: Ways of Accompaniment

classic work. Although written over 60 years ago, perhaps it is even truer in our day:

> "Woman's life today is tending more and more toward the state William James describes so well in the German word, 'Zerrissenheit—torn-to-pieces-hood'... On the contrary, she must consciously encourage those pursuits which oppose the centrifugal forces of today. Quiet times alone, contemplation, prayer.... What matters is that one be for a time inwardly attentive."[98]

Ruth:
"It was a very personal journey."

Ruth has been very involved with the catechesis for five years, and leading groups of older children, as well as during the most intense period of sacramental preparation. This, along with juggling professional (as a nurse) and personal demands (as a mother of two adopted boys), leaves little time for a deeply felt need. She again refers to herself as a "doer." This is a recurring theme for her. Evidently Ruth feels keenly the tension arising from the many demands in her life, and the need for quiet and meditation.

> "For me, coming to the course at night was quite stressful, especially at the time that we started the [research] group, and we were taking notes, and trying to focus in. It was at a time, too, when we were preparing for the First Communion [retreat]...and I was very anxious about that. So in a way, being asked to focus in on something really important in the group was a gift. Because after taking all these crazy notes and reading every word, I had that time after just to sit back and say, "What was important?" and

forcing [myself] to be quiet, and focusing in was very important. I was very late handing in my notes, and that turned out to be a gift, too. Because I had a lot of notes written, but they didn't have a lot of continuity at times. So in the summer I spent two or three days looking at the points I had made, sometimes knowing what I had meant, and sometimes not knowing, and going back to the notes and just spending a lot of meditative quiet time in going over it. And it really was a very positive experience, it was a very personal journey...things that maybe I hadn't heard, because I'm such a doer, writing down every single note. Sitting back and reading these carefully written notes at another time, I was able to experience it, and that was a very positive thing for me."

Ruth's words are instructive in light of the call for the laity "to work for the sanctification of the world from within, in the manner of leaven" (in the Second Vatican Council's Constitution on the Church, 31). In other words, she emphasizes the importance of taking the time to let the leaven work within oneself first in order to be fruitful in one's life and ministry.

Mary:
"Something small...but very significant."

Mary, also very active in her family and professional life, is without the luxury of much free time. This is especially so now because she is also involved in the sacramental retreat with children. Thus she mentions the tiredness she feels. Therefore, it is all the more striking that she appreciates the significance of the exercise of becoming attentive to what she had heard in the course.

Chapter Nine: Ways of Accompaniment

> "I found [the process] very beneficial.... I know how important it is that we try to reflect, and obviously observation is the key to the whole catechesis. And yet I know both of these are things that I hadn't really focused on...I found I was really tired at that time [of the course] but it was worth the effort [i.e. journaling]. And I found, too, that each evening I'd try to be thinking, to focus on that one thing that really hit me. And sometimes it would be something very small, but for that moment it was very, very significant. All the kinds of journaling were really good, because it really helped me to become a better observer. The same thing—if you make notes, evaluating how the class went, it helps you to remember better for the next time all the different things [one took note of re. the children]."

Important in this account is that what is remembered had deep meaning for her. Also, her words evoke the image of the Mustard Seed parable. Like that tiny seed, what is recalled about biblical and liturgical themes—even "something very small"—may have great meaning.

Domenica:
"Remembering, with joy."

Domenica's pressing teaching and family activities, in addition to her atrium involvement, means she arrived tired to the course. Thus her recall of what was a moment of revelation months earlier is striking. That is, the moment when she linked together the True Vine parable with the experience of listening to her daughter sing *"Vieni Gesu."* In synthesizing the experience as a whole, Domenica singles this out. And, once again on a deeply affective level, she speaks about the connection between the moment of nurturing, by means of hearing God's word (in the course), with a similar moment of being nurtured in hearing her daughter's song:

> "I really liked the idea of journaling because, when I went back after [seven] months and read my reflection I went, 'Wow! Did I write that?' I was amazed how deep it really was. Then reading it again I felt that joy, remembering. Then I went back to my [journal] notes; that's how I got back into it again [on the night before our reflection day]. And then I called my kids over, because one reflection reminded me of a song my daughter had been singing in Italian, and so I called both of my daughters over and said, 'Can you sing me that song again?' [It was] 'Come Lord Jesus, Remain in Me.' My daughter was preparing for First Holy Communion at her school and obviously her Italian teacher had taught them. I didn't know the words, but she had sung it for an hour in the van one day when we were going to see my parents in Guelph…So I called them last night and said, 'Come and sing me that song again.' So it's like recalling, remembering, with joy again, when reading that. If I was to take another course, I'd start journaling, just to internalize it; five minutes it took us at the end, but I needed that five minutes because by the time I got home, I was either too tired or had forgotten half of it. But that's what struck me."

It is worth noting that this memory is suffused with joy. Moreover, without the time to record it in her journal, Domenica may have missed the "Wow" experience expressed here.

Chapter Nine: Ways of Accompaniment

Wendy:
"Remembering God."

This is Wendy's third year in the atrium. It is only this year that she has assumed a more active role, and started presenting materials to the children. She has seen herself akin to the children in that she, too, was seeing presentations for the first time in the atrium. Now there is a desire to move to another level. She identifies her desire as becoming more of an "instrument." Wendy also highlights the importance of the "spiritual encounter."

> "My personal and spiritual development has been really challenged as a Christian. Since I began, this has been part of my Christian growth…I've identified with the feeling that I was one of the children watching these presentations for the first time, and then moving on from there to a place where I can actually take this information in and look at that information and then present it as an experience, offer it. I want to go from being a person who takes notes to some form of instrument.

> When you remember something, your own spiritual encounter with God or with a child, your spirit has changed; you have evolved from that point. So you bring something more, or you have something deeper, a depth to give. We always grow in that part of [ourselves] [in] the Holy Spirit through the gifts that are offered. Maybe it sounds kind of vague, but I'm a person who's always relied on writing things down. It's a big part of my expression as a person. Something I feel [is that] a catechist taking the course should journal at least once a week at some point, and share [it] with us, and the group will grow in some way."

Implications

The written journal exercise originated simply as an instrument with which to help the catechists to attend to their own experience. The reflection activity was just to provide an opportunity for expression in written form (journal). The importance of the reflection practice emerged as a constant refrain in the written evaluations of the catechists. Due to the inner growth ensuing from this simple attentiveness practice and the contemplative attitude it fostered, they all saw it as a valuable element in future courses. In addition, Kate suggests that a little reflection time follow directly after the presentation of the biblical/liturgical theme itself (rather than at the end of the course session, as it was done during this process).

> "After that moment [at the end of the course session], after you've experienced the presentation as it would be given to children, that would be a nice moment to journal. If [we] take that moment to journal, maybe out of that will come, when you're writing up the presentation later, some of the thoughts and meditation of your own moment. It would give the benefit that we all found from journaling—the going deeper. And also that wonderful moment—we would then remember [it] when we go back later to do the presentation [with children]."

Francesca suggests the value in sharing one's reflections with the larger group involved in the course.

> "I tend to be a very practical person, and…one of the things that strikes me is, if we hadn't had the opportunity to do this [journal], we would have missed so much. Not everyone who has taken the course is doing this, not everyone in the catechesis is doing this. The idea

of learning to observe and to be present to our own self spiritually, maybe in someway could be incorporated into some of the courses in the future… It's a very enriching process to be able to share with other people on that level, not [only] discussing presentations and 'how big should this be?' and "how many of those do you need?" and that kind of thing. It's a good kind of way to enter into it: it's very helpful, if we're going to live this."

To summarize, the importance the catechists ascribed to this simple exercise suggests two considerations relating to formation programmes: 1) The value of providing time for reflection (like the journal activity) and 2) The value of providing adequate time for an exchange among catechists about their reflections (on the experience in the course and with children).

Part 2: Observation

"It is necessary to be attentive to the greatness present in the child's littleness."[99]

Some Background

We have already seen that observation is one of the key elements in the formation of catechists. It is one way in which this catechesis applies some of Dr. Maria Montessori's educational principles. Montessori was insistent on the spiritual preparation of adults for their task as educators. The ability to observe children assumed a key role in her concept of the educator's training; "observation" is the word Montessori used to identify this skill. Additionally, Montessori attaches an explicitly religious aspect to discovering the child's nature by means of observation:

> "Now God has given to the child a nature of his own, and has fixed certain laws for his development... To discover the laws of the child's development would be the same thing as to discover the Spirit and Wisdom of God operating in the child."[100]

Speaking about the catechesis, Sofia states that "we are helping a vital process and not just an intellectual process." As such, observation becomes an essential element in the catechists' service.[101] In fact, it was only by observing children that Sofia and Gianna discerned vital indicators in their relationship with God. For example:

1) A great desire to continue to listen to specific themes and to continue their personal work with them on their own.

2) A profound sense of serene peace, of enchantment.

3) Some themes become part of the children themselves... as the result of a vital act, through which the child seems to have received something that corresponds... in a profound way, and of which the child has need...[102]

The Catechists' Experience

The importance of observation was not something new to these catechists. What was new was the specific emphasis it was given in our small group experience. For example, the catechists made a special commitment to a) write their observations of the children; and b) also to write their overall reflections about each atrium session.

In listening to the catechists during our reflection day, these

Chapter Nine: Ways of Accompaniment

two exercises assumed a significant place in their stories. We begin by noting some general characteristics that emerged. Then excerpts from their accounts will be presented, followed by some implications they contained.

About Observation

Observing children was generally seen as a valuable activity for all the catechists. As well, observation appears as having a formative role in refining their experience with children. All expressed a willingness to continue to work on their observation skills. Some suggested that this skill be investigated further (Ruth). Some want to exercise it more fully (Mary). Others are aware that this is a skill that needs development in their work with children (Eileen, Kate).

That said, observation appeared to be a complex experience for all the catechists. They are unanimous in seeing its value, but this activity posed challenges. All rate this in their written evaluations as a constructive component of the small group process. Yet, it also involved difficult aspects, in various forms and to different degrees.

The challenging aspect in observation seemed to arise from a kind of creative tension between two dimensions within it. One can be called the aesthetic dimension. That is, the art and craft involved in observation. The other can be called the ascetic dimension. That is, the discipline and effort involved in developing this skill.

The Art of Observation

The aesthetic element is apparent in the catechists' atrium accounts. The ability to observe appears as something of an art. It is recognized as an integral aspect of the skill and service of the catechist. Insofar as it is an art, it needs "honing," as one catechist says. That is, observation appears to be an activity that requires practice in order to refine one's skill and thus become more fruitful in one's service. As well, this aesthetic dimension is directly related to children. For instance, we will hear references to "choreographing" the time in the atrium with children.

The Task of Observation

On the other hand, the ascetic element is also apparent. Each catechist recognized that observing children requires effort. For each it is a demanding discipline, to varying degrees. These demands have particularities according to each catechist's personal style and strengths. As such, the demands can be quite distinct to the individual. Nevertheless, for all the catechists there is an invitation inherent in the observation activity. That is, they are aware of the need for growth in this area. Even so, there is openness and willingness in each catechist to persevere in what is evidently one of the more difficult dimensions of the catechist's service.

One final point. It seemed that the catechists who are most involved in this catechesis, in terms of duration and responsibility, are the ones who make clearest reference to the interplay between the aesthetic element and the ascetic element. That is, those who have had an amount of responsibility and many years in the atrium refer to observation in both terms: as an art/skill and as requiring effort/discipline. In order that this interplay may be seen more clearly, the catechists' accounts are sequenced in terms of these factors, namely the length of time and amount of involvement in the atrium with children.

The following excerpts are taken from catechists' oral accounts

Chapter Nine: Ways of Accompaniment

from our group reflection day. They were taped at the time and later transcribed in the form they appear here.

Eileen:
"It opened up something that's really of value."

In the course of her 11 years in the CGS, Eileen has already "done a lot of observing" of children. She refers to "choreographing the day," which indicates the aesthetic quality of this activity—almost like seeing catechesis as a dance. This dance calls for a certain quality of presence to children, and for her the challenging aspect is above all a practical one.

> "The observation in the atrium: for so many years, I've been in a position of doing the presentations and choreographing the day, and I think that for a lot of years, really [I'm] observing, but it's almost a very immediate observation. I don't know how much I'm carrying over, maybe one week to the next, but I don't know how much one year to the next... I think it's something that I always valued about the atrium... It [observation] was something that I really enjoyed; but my observation skills haven't really been honed. I'm observing, but I'm taking one particular thing and I'm looking at it carefully, but I think I'm just at that level where I'm taking it in. At times, I had a difficult time putting down exactly what I'm seeing, or what was being said. That I found to be a challenge... I can see the value of observation, but it's how to do it, how to be observing, and yet to be fully present with the children, so that you're completely with them. Yet, when you're in an observation mode—maybe it's just me—you're almost standing alongside. That to me was a bit of a challenge. In general, I enjoyed it, just

because it opened something up that's really of value. But it's just *how to do it*."

The practical concern is paramount here. Although observation is seen as a valuable practice, it seems that it may come in the way of being fully present to children. There is an additional concern as well. The term *observation* itself could seem an intrusion into the naturalness of the atrium experience. In consideration of this, when presenting the theoretical basis for this activity in the formation course it could be beneficial to explore the relaxed and receptive attitude represented in this passage by Josef Pieper:

> "What happens when we look at a rose? What do we do as we become aware of colour and form? Our soul is passive and receptive. We are, to be sure, awake and active, but our attention is not strained; we simply 'look'—insofar, that is, as we 'contemplate' it and are not already 'observing' it (for 'observing' implies that we are beginning to count, to measure and to weigh up). Observation is a tense activity... To contemplate, on the other hand, to 'look' in this sense, means to open one's eyes receptively to whatever offers itself to one's vision, and the things seen enter into us, so to speak, without calling for any effort or strain on our part to possess them."[103]

Certainly the practice of observation is not meant to be a "tense activity." Therefore, highlighting the contemplative attitude, as conveyed by Pam Moore's following term "savoring," may disclose new meanings implicit in the word "observation." This term also minimizes the risk of it being perceived as distancing from, rather than an enhancing of, the relationship with children:

Chapter Nine: Ways of Accompaniment

"I also see savouring the child's wisdom as a gentler, less arduous angle on our task of observing the child. Savoring implies prolonged admiration and continual rumination. When we savor something, we take the experience with us, cherishing the initial moment of delight well into the future."[104]

Francesca:
"I know what their hunger is."

After 10 years in the CGS, Francesca is obviously familiar with the practice of observation in the atrium. Her account alludes to the art involved in this exercise. She too employs the image of choreography in relation to her role with children. For her, the particular value in this activity resides in the remembrance of important moments in the atrium with children. There is a problematic aspect, however, requiring a "long-range" approach.

> "I found the part about observing the children really hard, really difficult, because I guess being busy doing the things, you don't observe them in the same way; you're concerned about the choreographing. I'm not really good at writing things out when it happens, and I tend to think I'll remember that, and then I forget it. It's almost like if you're sure you'll remember it, that's when you forget it...So the parts with the children were very important....I was just very free about it. With the children...I know what their hunger is already, and their response to the different things and their readiness for it and afterwards, as things go for several years afterwards. I've seen children afterwards saying, when we talk about the First Communion group... 'Are you going to do this?' 'Are you going to

do that?'…it's like, 'Oh you're so lucky, I wish I could come again.' That's a response that you don't see when the children are there at that moment…To observe the children, I don't think I could have done it faithfully if I had just looked at the time of the presentation. It's the time before and the time afterwards, and the impact it had on their lives. You don't immediately see the long range picture, but over time, you do see…."

Francesca is attentive to the children's "hunger." She also admits to the difficulty that the activity of observation entails for her. Here one senses the ascetic element, the discipline that is involved in this dimension of catechesis with children. Nevertheless, there is an undercurrent of joy derived from observing the children's responses, which recalls Dr. Maria Montessori's words about the "joyous observer":

> "…the first step…is to shed omnipotence and to become a joyous observer. If the [educator] can really enter into the joy of seeing things…many delights are reserved for [that person]."[105]

Montessori's words connote a self-emptying attitude, but she continues by saying that this "renunciation of power and authority" is "to renounce lesser for greater joys." Perhaps accenting the quality of joyous observation would highlight the enjoyment possible in exercising this skill, and thus help to balance the difficulty it may entail.

Kate:
"I see it…as a very important activity for myself."

Kate's nine years as co-founder and co-director of her parish atrium centre has not dimmed her sense of humour. Her

Chapter Nine: Ways of Accompaniment

account is light-hearted, causing laughter in the group. While affirming the importance of this activity for herself, she is clear about the difficulties involved in its practice. Her account is multi-layered. On the personal level, observation constitutes for her a "critical, analytical" disposition. On the level of ministry, observation heightens her need for "meditation" as a catechist. On the practical level, she prefers "group sharing" as a way to develop the skill further.

> "Observing in the atrium, I likewise found some difficulties in that. I tend to observe situations in a very analytical, critical framework. And so it's very easy for me to see all the things that don't work and that need improving. It's very hard for me to see things that are positive. This made me more aware; I became even more aware of that. I mean, if I only did that, I'm sure I would leave the catechesis! Because I would say, 'There's so much that needs to be done!' [Laughter.] That was hard…With the older group I was trying to take down notes; because usually I was rushing out afterwards, and then to find a moment to remember it is hopeless…On the other hand, I see it for *myself* as a very important activity that I sort of still haven't learned to do. And that's to be able to observe and see the positive, and see what's happening with the children. Because I find the work is sustaining when we have adult interaction, when we have courses, when we have ways that nurture ourselves. But just being in the atrium with the children, unless I step back and somehow meditate on that, or share that with other catechists, and take the time to do that, I find just being there for that chunk of time, for myself, it isn't enough. I think it's still something I personally need to develop a lot more."

Like Leaven

In a conversation with Renilde Montessori, I mentioned Kate's reference to "step back and meditate." Renilde responded:

> "To me, observation and meditation are akin. [Also] I see observation as a scientific enchantment. Enchantment calls forth a growth, a flowering of the personality. Observation is a living experience. You are taking in the life of another element—a child—and you lose yourself in this…in awe and wonder."

Kate's account also emphasizes the contribution that dialogue with other catechists could bring to this spiritual practice.

> "While I find it impossible to reflect on what my time with the children means to me—I think it is possible to do it over a longer time period—like a 'semester' or year of working with the children meant to me. Even this reflection, however, for me personally would be greatly assisted by more direct questions or by a group discussion which would trigger my own responses."

Renilde, during that same conversation, offered a helpful insight in light of orienting the adult with regards to the practice of observation. That is, learning how children observe:

> "I find it difficult when people ask, 'Give me guidelines for observation.' How can I give you guidelines for living? Children are observers who observe because they need to know, because that is part of their self-instruction. Children are the best teachers of observation. They observe with total absorption; it's vital for them."

Chapter Nine: Ways of Accompaniment

Ruth:
"Just doing"..."feelings and internalizing."

From the very start of her initiation into the catechesis, Ruth has been very involved in children's groups, including the older children's retreats. Perhaps this is what is reflected in her concern about "just doing," a thread running throughout her reflections. She, too, highlights that group sharing is personally nurturing and professionally formative.

> "With the children, it was difficult observing. Because I don't think I'd ever done that before, and I didn't know how to do it... I can't remember things very long; it's just for a few minutes! I didn't try to write out the whole sheet, but I did take notes throughout the classes that we had. Sometimes they were good, sometimes not. But I did find it very positive having the opportunity to speak with other catechists after [the atrium session]: 'Did you hear that?' Then I would realize things from her eyes [other catechist], from what she observed, that maybe I hadn't seen, that maybe I hadn't observed. We had the chance to talk and I think that is really a positive tool that we should begin to investigate. Because I agree with Kate that without that, we are just doing, and trying to make it better. The logistics are maybe really reinforced, whereas our observations and our feelings and our internalizing don't get as much of a chance at this time. You have to do it at that time, right at that moment that it's happening or maybe right after...."

Another important point in Ruth's excerpt is the contemplative dimension embedded in this catechesis. It can be seen in her former references to "being" verses "doing," as well as here in the dissatisfaction with the "logistics" of action over the attention to "feeling." Her intentionality about "internalizing" the experience, in contrast to mere efficiency or "just doing... it better," coupled with her mention of the time spent in the summer "re-reading" and meditating on her journal, point to the contemplative element, which is apparent in all these accounts.[106]

Mary:
"I still struggle."

After four years in the atrium, this year is the first that Mary takes an active role during the children's retreat. As she describes it, her primary challenge in observing is very personal. At the same time, she appreciates the attention given to this practice during our small group experience.

> "I really, really did appreciate it. Not only in, as you [Eileen] say, picking that key point from the meeting that we had or the [course] session, but also in the atrium. I mean I'm still very much in awe of that, because I tend to be the type, well, my family can ask me to pass them the salt and I wouldn't even hear them! I'm often in another world. And I still struggle with that to a certain extent. So it's definitely not one of my strong points, to be really, really observant to the very subtle things, but I can certainly start."

Mary's words illustrate the radical nature of attentive observation in light of the personal call it represents. They speak about her desire to be attentive, as well as the personal cost involved in it. In fact, Bernard Lonergan, the Canadian theologian quoted earlier, explored the various movements in the conversion process, and stated that the first movement is

Chapter Nine: Ways of Accompaniment

to pay attention:

> "At the core of people's experience of flow—feeling most alive and absorbingly engaged—is the phenomenon of attention. To enter the optimal experience of *flow*, people must concentrate in a special and enriching way… We call this ability *paying* attention because it is neither spontaneous nor free. Paying attention is a learned discipline and a developed skill." (author's emphasis)[107]

Thus it could be said that to be observant/attentive is to engage in the call to conversion. Perhaps becoming more aware of the conversion dimension inherent within the activity of observation may be an encouragement to embrace this activity as a spiritual practice.

Domenica:
"It furthered my relationship with God."

Domenica's excerpt is infused with emotion. Even recalling the atrium sessions evoked deep feelings. She relates the source of this emotion to being able to see the children's "connectedness to God," especially in prayer.

> "I wanted to say about the focusing—that worked. And then we had to write it down, and I did that. I loved that [observation], because it really made me focus on how the kids were. But a lot of the times I felt schizophrenic because I was just seeing some of these presentations for the first time, so I was feeling, I guess, what they were feeling, yet I had to observe what they were feeling! It was hard to focus in, but I tell you, I rejoiced in the joy and peace of seeing some

of those kids in the prayer room, their connectedness to God, and the whole spirit touched me [tears]. I found it furthered my relationship with God, and it gives me joy to be there with the kids, and watching them, because their relationship is probably greater than mine is, and I'd like to get it back to that plane."

There are two points of specific interest in Domenica's account. The first, once again, is the child's ability to be a source of formation for adults. The other point is how children can call forth a desire in the adult to seek that quality of relationship they manifest with God, or, "getting it back to that plane," as Domenica expresses it. After listening to the group during this reflection day, Br. Ignatius noted in the catechists' accounts

"the wonderful modelling of what exactly this catechesis is all about: the child becomes the 'formator' together with the catechists; the children are the teachers."

Wendy:
"I am growing."

As mentioned earlier until this year Wendy's role in the atrium has been, predominantly one of observer. The two previous years allowed her a prolonged period of attentiveness. The contemplative approach is evident in her excerpt here. There is a recurrence of her understanding of observation as "witnessing," suggesting an experience for her that is similar to prayer. Wendy's reflection recalled this penetrating insight:

"The adult who prays will begin to see the child differently, which alone can initiate change. In prayer one also begins to see how children play a role in the formation of adults… We also begin to notice how close children are to the praise of God."[108]

Chapter Nine: Ways of Accompaniment

Nonetheless, Wendy also indicates the problematic aspect in this practice, identified in her propensity for analysis and compartmentalization.

> "In this work, we watch the children grow, but we ourselves also grow. I remember when we first began to study observation…this question just popped into my mind: What is the difference between observation and Christian witnessing? I was trying to separate the two, trying to look at them as two different things and then over time, I realized that they're often intertwined and you can't really separate [them]. Then you watch a child pray, watch them light candles, or set up the altar… I saw such a love and a diligence [that] they poured into it. I thought, what am I seeing? Am I observing? Am I witnessing? Then I realized that… I think I was being too analytical in my approach, and I was trying to just compartmentalize things and experiences, and really many things are not like that. We experience many things at one time… And I have to learn to allow these experiences, just to enjoy them for what they are, and then later to give thanks that I was there and to ask the Lord to be with me the next time so I can do more for the children. My desire is always to do more for them, because I love being there with them and watching them. [God] puts us in a position where we are witnessing the child going through changes in life… Every time I go to the atrium it's never the same as the last one, it's always different in some way. So, for me too, I am growing…because [my] perceptions change as I go on. I think writing it down just gives you a chance to go back and to learn, because we forget things and [it helps] to re-enter. It's to allow God to come back to you."

One implication here is the attitude of openness to receive, with gratitude, what children have to offer the adult, and thus to focus on the all-important reality of gift.

Another implication is the element of enjoyment this practice can hold for the adult. Keeping the element of joy and enjoyment in the foreground might provide a counter-balance to the effort this practice requires. Observing children may be approached as an opportunity, as Wendy puts it, "to allow God to come back" to oneself. Moreover, as Sofia writes:

> "if we let ourselves become involved in the Word of God with children we too…can discover or rediscover some fundamental values of the religious life which I would synthesize primarily as essentiality and enjoyment—the presence of God in our life as the source of deep enjoyment."[109]

Attentiveness/Observation in Ministry with Children

	Attentiveness as Invitation to: Aestheticism	Attentiveness as Invitation to: Asceticism	Attentiveness as Call to: Conversion
Eileen	• choreographing the day… something I've always valued about the atrium	• I can see the value… observation skills haven't really been honed	• but it's how to do it? • how to do it so that you're completely with them [the children].
Francesca	• concerned about choreographing • seeing the long-range picture	• really difficult • I tend to forget	• how to remember…?
Kate	• a very important activity	• difficulties… • analytical, critical	• to see the positive something I personally need to develop
Ruth	• positive tool • "Did you see…hear that?"	• difficult…remembering observation skills need honing	• how to do it…? • to attend to own "feelings" and internalizing"
Mary	• really did appreciate it	• struggle…I'm often in another world	• I can certainly start…to be really observant to the very subtle things
Domenica	• enjoyed that • I rejoiced in the joy and peace of their [children] connectedness to God.	• Hard	• to focus in on how the kids were
Wendy	• observation as Christian witnessing…being there with children and watching them	• Too analytical in approach • Trying to compartmentalize	• to allow these experiences • to enjoy them for what they are

Chapter Ten:
Journey Together

Some months later we held our final reflection day as a way of bringing our time together as a small group to a close (in January of the following year).

Once again, Brother Ignatius served as our facilitator. He opened the day with a gathering prayer, which included two scripture passages from the book of Wisdom. The first passage describes the nature of Wisdom: "Wisdom, the fashioner of all things..." (Wisdom 7: 22; 8: 1). The second passage contains Solomon's prayer for Wisdom: "O God of my ancestors and Lord of mercy..." (Wisdom 9: 1-6; 9-11). Then Br. Ignatius offered two points for the catechists' reflection. First, he invited all

> "to find an image or symbol that connects with what we are feeling; to find and to speak that image that is characteristic of me in my life at this moment."

The first part of this chapter looks at the image which represents each of the catechists' experience; the excerpts below are taken from their verbatim accounts. These images are also presented in an overview chart at the end of this part (see Catechists' Images).[110] Part two of this chapter presents the catechists' response to the second point of reflection offered by Brother Ignatius. He invited everyone to bring their experience of the overall process

Chapter Ten: Journey Together

"more completely into dialogue with…the place where you converse with God, the place where 'Wisdom' dwells, by reflecting on the experience using whatever means you wish: thoughts, feelings, images, metaphors, hopes and desires."

Part I: Images of Growth

Before presenting the catechists' excerpts, three common threads in these images will be noted.

The first thread is the preponderance of biblical imagery, especially Christological. This reveals the power of scripture, the True Vine parable in particular. It also highlights the impact of the reflection activity. The second thread is the mention of the Holy Spirit. For example: as in the "gifts of the Spirit", as "sap," as "Wisdom", and more allusively, as in Francesca's "white egg" metaphor below. The third thread woven into each of these accounts is their relationship with children.

Eileen:
"The True Vine"

"The image of the True Vine… I think of that remaining, that just being—how we are with the children…because we are just remaining, and we are with the children in this way. That really sets us apart; that's not something that we can 'take', and that we can 'learn', and we can "teach" that to the children. I think that it has always a double edge to it; because it makes it much simpler in so many ways, yet much…larger because it's so deep. Or communicating to others, it can only be done this way. From what I've seen for myself and for other people, this is a common thread: that everyone says this is 'a part of their life'... So I think that the image of the True Vine is very powerful...."

Francesca:
"It's wonderful...the white egg."

"The first image that I got was one of a white egg... and I'm on the inside, and God is on the outside, and God looks at the egg... It's like God pecks from the outside, and gently taps on this egg, and knows that I'm ready, but gently taps... It's [a] very nurturing, very comfortable kind of feeling. It's not coming from me trying to break out, but it's like God inviting me to come out... So I see this white egg, but it's not just me; if I'm a white egg, then everyone's a white egg and so are all the children, and it's that kind of delicacy that we need to be able to honour the children, honour each other, and to just allow that gentle tapping. And then one day I'll get out! And it's that kind of moment, it's wonderful...the white egg."

Kate:
"Just being with Wisdom."

"I have an image...and it says that 'Wisdom permeates everything', and lives 'in everything'; and then the last line was, 'God loves nothing so much as the person who lives with Wisdom.' It just resonated within me when we talk about the sap of the True Vine and how wisdom is here and God loves nothing so much as us just being with Wisdom. And I think it also resonates with me in the catechesis, in that there is a real trust in Wisdom: that God is with us, God is within us. And that by being in this way is good, and that we don't have to be looking for all the results, or trying to measure, or trying to see if either ourselves or the children…are 'accomplishing'. But that is a gift in itself that we don't have to do anything else."[111]

Ruth:
"When Mary said, 'Yes'."

"What I was thinking of is [the phrase] 'enter into'… And I think as catechists, that's what we have done; we have entered into the process of the journey together and this is quite similar to what Eileen was saying [concerning the True Vine]. It permeates our life and we've entered into it together on this journey. It's similar to me—this parable—when Mary said, 'Yes.' When she said 'Yes,' she entered into, and nothing was the same again. So I feel that's the kind of journey when we do presentations: we invite the children to enter in with us, sharing with Wisdom, sharing God's love on the journey of life."

Mary:
"Illuminating, like the light."

"Light…to have illuminated so much in me, and so many truths have become clear, and even so many connections and interweavings…that have become clear. And just in preparing to make a presentation to the children, and in thinking about how to best allow them to, I guess to see that light…to think about staying with the essence and the heart is important too. It's helped me even in the atrium. And in general too, to be able to communicate better… And for it to grow and to deepen, because of the way that we're sort of guided to convey the information and…to look for the heart, the essence, and not go off on a tangent, and not to focus in too many directions. But just to [be] clear, crystal clear. I see that as something very illuminating, like the light."

Domenica:
"Gifts of the Spirit."

"I thought of when we used to do [the presentation of] the gifts of the Holy Spirit: knowledge and wisdom… And then I guess I realize that Wisdom is like a Spirit, a presence that is inside us, or close to us, so that we will know how to share that knowledge with the children, and with each other, of what we've learned in the catechesis… Looking at the first reading from Wisdom: that's inside us, the presence of our Good Shepherd, and the love of the whole catechesis; the love that we want to share with each other and with the children, and the love that we feel for each other here."

Wendy:
"What is the 'sap'?"

"I chose the True Vine also… What is the 'sap' of the True Vine? The 'sap' is the Holy Spirit. That's what I think about…and I really enjoy being with [young] people a lot and working with them in this way. It's wonderful to see the Spirit come out [of children]. One of my favourite pieces of scripture is 'God is Spirit.' And I think about those three words sometimes and I often think that simple words say so much."

Chapter Ten: Journey Together

In concluding this section, we note a reference to children in all these personal images. That is, the children's presence appears to be integrated into the catechists' images (their presence is highlighted in the chart below). This recalls an earlier theme of "remembering one's spiritual encounter with God…and children," as one catechist expressed it. The following excerpt by Domenica makes explicit the presence of children as an important factor in the formation process. In considering the catechists' images once again, it appears that this catechesis facilitates a mutually formative experience, one in which both adult and child are sources of nurturance, one for the other.

> "I think we learned how to sensitize ourselves, [to be] more sensitive to what was happening in class, in taking the course, and then when we're in there [atrium] watching the kids… Also [to be] more appreciative of God, first of all; every time I came to the course I learned how to appreciate and know [that] all the time he is there and to remember he's there… Because with our busy lives, who's got time? We have to discipline ourselves and say, 'Yes, let's take a moment to think about this'… And [to] sensitize [ourselves] to the kids too, watching what's happening, through all the senses, in their lives and what's in them."

Catechists' Images

	Image	Biblical Allusion	Presence of/ relationship to/ children
Eileen	• "the True Vine is very powerful" • "being… remaining"	John 15:1-11	remaining—and we are with the children in this way That being… how we are with the children
Francesca	• "the white egg" prayer image: "Create anew"; "like giving birth"	God: ("as a hen…" brooding over "chick" (Matthew 23:37.) Divine inbreathing at creation (Genesis 2:7) and rebirth (John 3:8)	"then everyone is a white egg, so are all the children"
Kate	• "sap of the True Vine" • being with "Wisdom"	John 15: 1-11 Wisdom 7: 24, 28 (as Spirit)	being in this way is a gift; we don't have to measure ourselves or children, or to see what we or children are accomplishing
Ruth	• "enter into": Mary's "Yes"… • like the True Vine	Annunciation: Luke 1:35-8; (the Spirit's overshadowing presence) John 15	we invite the children to enter in with us sharing with Wisdom, God's love

Chapter Ten: Journey Together

Mary	• "light… illuminating crystal clear"	God (Jesus) as "light": John 8:12; 1 John 4:9 "let there be light" (Spirit's hovering) Genesis 1:3	how to best allow children to see that light
Domenica	• gifts of the Holy Spirit… knowledge and wisdom…	"The Spirit of the Lord…a spirit of wisdom… knowledge" (Isaiah 11:2 ff.)	the love that we want to share with each other and with the children
Wendy	• "sap of the True Vine" • "sap is the Holy Spirit" • God is Spirit	John 15 John 4:24	It's wonderful to see the Spirit come out of the children

Like Leaven

Part 2: Growing in Community

In response to the second point of reflection that Brother Ignatius offered, the catechists described their overall impression of the preceding months. Their responses are presented verbatim here.

In each summary statement of the catechist's involvement in this experience, different aspects emerged in terms of growth in community. Clearly, one common theme was the place that sharing one's experience and faith holds in providing hope and strength to go forward in ministry. This reflects Henri Nouwen's insight:

> "We have a mission to fulfill…but first we have to listen to what others have to say. Then our stories can be told and bring joy… The community of faith is the place where many stories about the way of Jesus are being told."[112]

Another dominant theme is the importance of the role of community in giving impetus and encouragement with respect to one's service as catechist with children.[113]

Eileen:
"Taking things to another level."

"It just struck me when we were talking…of taking things to another level; and so almost taking this now to the children, and our experience with the children. Because I think that this is so valuable, and we're all speaking really, as we should be, from a personal point of view. But also I think it would be so valuable to look at even the little observations that we have made, go back in our notes with the children, and maybe it would

Chapter Ten: Journey Together

be more of a dialogue there, and how people see things with the children. Not so much people's opinions or to compare notes, but it would just be to take this and [ask]: 'How are we with the children?' It just seems like it would be a natural progression."

Francesca:
"Go back and be real."

"I think one of the bonuses of doing the First Communion and Reconciliation [retreat] with the children is that through the work and everything else, at the end you have this real sense of community… the community sense is so strong. They're so excited, they're so involved with each other and all sorts of new relationships evolve. Almost to the point that you almost hear them saying, 'Can't we just keep this going?'…I've just seen over the years, the kids stay together, connected, and so they kind of live in both worlds: that sense of the community built in a retreat, an intimate experience, yet they still work with the other people. I think that's probably the reality of what we have to do. We've had this intimate moment, and we need to be able to stay connected within that, but also go back and be real with other people, and the kids, the programme… Sometimes you don't think you're speaking the same language as anybody else. And you really wonder, do people understand what you're trying to say? Sometimes you wonder, and you really need to connect with people…and just know that someone understands the language you're speaking, and what you're trying to do. It's really, really, important."

Like Leaven

Kate:
"To take another step."

"In my group [with children] I really need a kind of support that this kind of sharing brings. I guess in some ways it's affirming each of our journeys. And I find that in the atrium, you know we have each other, but we don't spend a lot of time with each other talking [about] our journeys. Because even, as I said earlier, the idea of remaining on the vine, I'm so easily distracted by the things that I didn't do [in the atrium] to make things happen… If I just try to remember why I'm there, and the way you [Eileen] describe how we are with the children—we're all on the vine together. And I love your image, Francesca, of the gentle pecking on the egg and maybe that's what we're doing with the children too—letting the light shine in. And so to be able to take that moment and to try to center myself again, before I start [with the children]… So I think for me this really… gives me the hope and the energy to take another step on the journey."

Ruth:
"To stay on our journey."

"Being here is very empowering, in that—as you [Wendy] say—we're speaking the same language. We're communicating together, and…one of the most positive things was speaking together [as catechists] after the atrium classes and sharing, like we are doing here. So I think it would be wonderful if we could continue to do it. And in some way we need to do it in order to keep the energy, and to keep positive, and to stay on our journey, on the road together."

Chapter Ten: Journey Together

Mary:
"Common thread, common root."

"That's sort of what I feel too…but [it is] to actually hear that, and to communicate that to each other, and to realize that it's been a very important part of all of our lives… I think it would be nice perhaps, now that we're not meeting together every week like we did, to find a different format. It would be nice perhaps to try to continue to communicate and to share with each other. The group reflection day was important to put words and expression to something so very important to us, yet not easily understood by those not involved in the catechesis. It was good, reaffirming, to be understood and to share our experiences with their common thread, our feelings with their common root."

Domenica:
"Another step in our relationship."

"I feel like I'm privileged to be in this group, just from the fact that everyone seems to be very bold, very intimate with their spirituality in telling how they're touched… In doing so, I think we affirm the catechesis, we affirm ourselves; and hearing someone else from the group, or maybe we get some insights into another section, or another idea… That's another step in our relationship with each other."

Wendy:
"To share…on an ongoing basis."

"During the course, one of the things that meant a lot to me was the sense of unity among us as catechists.

Being in the room together, I really felt the presence of the Holy Spirit... I very much enjoy the fellowship with other people who are involved in this work... I think as a group we shared something here that we don't share with others... I think it's very good for us to continue to share it all on an ongoing basis. We are able to relate to each other here. We have a certain companionship... we share an understanding of each other's perspectives, and that comes from what we've learned... You know it's like it becomes a language. It's like your own prayer; in a way we have a language by which we understand [each other]... I listen to someone else and I know we are connected, and then I go back to the atrium... You can't measure these things, but you can give them. And I think it's just part of the life God has given us."

Summary

In summation, once again we note in these excerpts the movements highlighted earlier: communion with God, community, ministry or mission (in Chapter 8).

Participating as a member of a small community, gathered explicitly to share their faith journey, affirmed the role of community as a personal source of sustenance. Community is also a crucial element in empowering catechists to continue in their ministry. The two elements of community and ministry, and the interconnection between them, is highlighted in schematic chart form below. This movement has been described as a Eucharistic movement:

> "The movement flowing from the Eucharist is the movement from communion to community to ministry. Our experience of communion first sends us to our

Chapter Ten: Journey Together

brothers and sisters to share with them our stories and build with them a body of love. Then, as community, we can move in all directions and reach out to all people."[114]

This Eucharistic movement is the foundation of what Sofia describes as the "spirituality of the catechists of the Good Shepherd":

> "[the] Eucharist is a pivot in the religious experience of the child and, if this is true, the Eucharist is also the pivot of the spiritual life of the catechist. If we dare speak about a spirituality of the catechists of the Good Shepherd, we must speak about a Eucharistic spirituality."[115]

	Growth in Community: Shared Faith and Praxis	Towards Ministry: Future Orientation
Eileen	• Valuable from a personal point of view. • More dialogue on how people see things with the children.	Go to another level; taking this now to the children and how we are with children; seems a natural progression.
Francesca	• Intimate moment…we need to stay connected within that. • Understanding what you're doing; speaking the same language.	But also to go back and be real with other people and the kids and the programme.
Kate	• The support this kind of sharing brings. • How and what we're doing with children.	Gives me hope and energy to take another step on the journey.
Ruth	• Empowering…we're communicating. • Speaking the same language; sharing like we are here.	Need to continue [sharing] to keep energy to stay on our journey, on the road together.
Mary	• We feel similarly, to hear that, to communicate that. It's [atrium/children] a very important part of our lives.	Try to continue to communicate and to share that with each other.
Domenica	• Intimate with our spirituality. • Affirm ourselves; get insights and ideas.	That's another step in our relationship.
Wendy	• Unity and fellowship. I felt the presence of the Holy Spirit. • To talk about the work; sharing, understanding of perspective and language.	Continue to share on an ongoing basis.

Epilogue:
The Good Shepherd Catechesis: As a Way

By way of context, we recall that a final reflection day served as the concluding moment of our journey together. We also recall that Brother Ignatius offered all the catechists the opportunity to look back at their experience as a whole.

After that final gathering, there was a long period in which I re-read and re-played the catechists' words from the beginning of our small research group process to this concluding moment. During that period, a motif became increasingly discernible throughout their accounts, namely, of this catechesis as a "way."

Much as a prism's light is refracted in different hues, each catechist had a unique understanding of this catechesis. Or, as one of the catechists remarked, "We [are] walking our way through it as we [are] doing it." The summary statements of their understanding of the catechesis are excerpted here verbatim (and already previewed in chart format in the Introduction).

Lastly, a personal retrospective follows their excerpts. It highlights some principle aspects found in their overall experience, and includes references to the influence of the children's presence in their accounts.

The Catechesis as a Way

Eileen:
A way of...being.

"I think of that *remaining*, that just *being*.... Really, that seems to be what sets this apart from other religious education programs or teaching, that we are together on this vine with the children; it's not just 'teaching'. And it's almost a prerequisite that we have this experience of the [True Vine] before we can make these announcements to the children. Because it's not so much the words we're using, it's how we're making the announcement.... After so many years, you hear it more and more, 'This has *touched* me, this has *affected* me,' from new people just being introduced or hearing it for the first time—this phenomenon of this *being*. This isn't surprising for us, but if you look at [other] kinds of education programs, anything that deals with children, you usually don't take that [personal] step... it's usually only, 'Yeah, I can see how this would work with the children.'"

Francesca:
A way of...prayer.

"Basically I ended up coming up with a prayer at the end of the summer: it was God, breathing new life into us every minute, every day, every breath you take... because it's something you can do anywhere, and at any minute, and at any time. In joy, or in stress, or in anything, you can do this. I think it's kind of like giving birth, as you do these different breathing things. It's really had an impact and I've seen things happen in my own life which were really great, that I know wouldn't have happened otherwise. Even things like with my own parents or different struggles, that before I would have said, 'Oh, this is going to be awful!' and I just go: 'Create anew in me God, this instant, this minute.' Or else as I was going through situations: 'Create this new in me,' and then breathe it in and let it out and it was wonderful.…. That's what I will always remember from that moment…this prayer that I was able to do that suited me and my breathing."

Kate:
A way of…fire.

"The process of sharing our vision, hopes, experiences and struggles in this ministry helps me to clarify what I am doing and why. It also provides the support I personally need to continue. There is something about when we commit ourselves. If it's too easy, we tend not to put as much effort into it as well. I mean, I think back on 'how the heck did I take the [summer] courses?' Those summers I had two very young babies and I went full time for three weeks. How could I do that? Part of it is a willingness, that's a huge part of it, as much as ability. If you're really caught on fire by what it is, it's amazing what one can do. Sometimes today I think, 'Where is that fire?'…. I need to be brought back to those moments of joy and fire. And that's so important if I'm going to stay in the work."

Ruth:
A way…with children.

"The atrium, the catechesis of the Good Shepherd

has changed my life. I notice it especially with my children, and with other children, and it's in the way of the presentation, the way you present things, the way you speak with the children, the way you respect each moment, and what is happening. The way you let that moment happen."

Mary:
A way…to find God.

"I do feel very differently about [the catechesis] than I do anything else I've been involved in. I do feel much more that it has become a part of me, and in some way that I would always carry this with me.… There would always be something in me that would want to try to find that, or develop that, or be a part of that. I do feel that it's very special, and it has become a part of my life in a deeper way than I would have thought. It just sort of happened without me realizing it. But it's true! I think in my own life, my relationship with God came through times of unhappiness, and searching, and struggle; and on one hand, we hear so many people [who] seem to feel that that's almost the only way people find God. And I just think that anyone can try to show this way to others. I just think that this is another way to find God. It's not the way of pain, it's not the way of suffering, it's just the natural way of sort of starting at the beginning. I think it's a beautiful way."

Domenica:
A way of…peace and joy.

"I'd like to say that when I started the catechesis I felt

Epilogue: The Good Shepherd Catechesis: As a Way

like I was that 3 year-old child sitting in that chair listening. That isn't to make me feel smaller, but to dignify how I felt about being there. I like the focusing, as we did it as an activity. I think I focused because I'd go home the next day and talk to [friend]. So I was internalizing it.... I think that the Spirit was flowing to the children, and from the child in me, and I wanted to share that same feeling with a good friend. And internalizing it as I verbalized it to her, I guess it sparked something. But I saw the peace and joy, not only in the children, but in many other catechists that were there [in the atrium], and I wanted that peace and joy in my heart."

Wendy:
A way of...relationship

"When I first discovered the catechesis, it was like falling in love for me. And now I find myself [more] practical...reality has changed for me. I think when I look at myself, it's like I started a new relationship with God, and in this relationship, somehow I felt a great sense of love.... Somewhere along the line, I feel myself settling down somehow inside...whereas before I was 'à la carte'. I love it! Something is happening to me, and I'm just beginning this past year to really experience it. I think what's happened is, as I watch these children grow, and go through their motions, of going from three years old to making First Reconciliation and First Communion, [I am] seeing that life changes. I think one of the reasons for me this work is so real is because it isn't all in the head; it's something that we do with our hands, with all of our senses.... So it's really been interesting. Yes: fall in love, and be in awe,

> but also use your judgement, use all of your senses. Because, basically, I'm a dreamer type of person. It's really developed my relationship with children in a way that I never even knew existed.... It's something I believe I can't even completely articulate, but I have a different viewpoint and a different way of relating to children."

In addition, what also emerged from the catechists' description is that this catechesis is also a paschal way. Many strains of the paschal mystery are perceptible in all their stories. And noteworthy in all of them is the dynamism of hope.

This is exemplified in the following series of excerpts gleaned from Francesca's accounts over the course of our time together. Especially in the struggle, the dynamism of hope sustains continued commitment on the journey of faith as well as mission.

April

> "Sure it's fine to [proclaim] things to the children! Hmmm, great!! But then when you hear it yourself, 'Remain on the vine', I'm going, 'I really sometimes didn't want to remain on the vine! I just want to go.' When you actually take this catechesis and walk through it in your moments in your life, through your ups and downs and your crises, it's like a true test. And I know where the struggle's coming from—it's me.... I mean these maxims could basically shape my life if I took them seriously."

September

"Out of this, I hadn't intended to develop a prayer style for me ... I think it's kind of like giving birth ... 'Create anew in me God'."

January

"The reality is ... [I] guess you go through different stages. In the catechesis you go through different rhythms....

We're the ones who got really involved and committed. You go through that process, go through great lengths and you do it.... It's not: 'Here it is on a silver platter.' There is a sense of mission."

Personal Retrospective

Finally, all the catechists' accounts were viewed in an overarching sense. So, as a concluding note, this retrospective will track certain aspects that were clarified in this overall view. This recapitulation will be illustrated with two diagrams.

With regard to the primary phase of the pastoral experience, the relationship with God was most significant, as nourished by the biblical and liturgical sources. It also highlighted the manner in which the encounter with God was facilitated by means of the methodological elements: 1) the materials concretizing the theological themes; and 2) their mode of presentation. A diagram was then presented (Fig. 1, chapter 6) to indicate: 1) the power of the content (biblical and liturgical) in initiating their encounter with God, and 2) the impact of the methodology (presentation and materials) in mediating it.

We mentioned how these sources led them to a deepening movement towards prayer and meditation, thus pointing to the potentially transformative dimension in this catechesis. I say "potentially" transformative because, it "incorporate[s] the radically transforming possibilities of grace."[116] Even more, "potentially" is also meant to indicate that:

> All human education can only provide subject matter… but it cannot force acceptance or imitation… Nature and the subject's freedom of will impose limits on spiritual formation. But there is *one* Educator for whom these limits do not exist: God, who has given nature, can transform it…" (author's emphasis)[117]

This can be developed further, in view of the understanding about the course and the ministry with children that came from the catechists' accounts. We recall that special emphasis given to the two exercises of attentiveness—reflection and observation. By these means various levels of personal involvement seemed to open within the catechists. Their images for the experience as a whole, given here and in the previous chapter, add insight into this deepening dynamic, which is abbreviated in the following five-part synthesis.

1) **Identification:** The process appears to have been initiated by listening to and identifying significant aspects in the course and atrium experiences.

2) **Personalization:** The attentiveness exercises allowed time and space to relate that to one's own life, and to record what had personal impact for them.

3) **Internalization:** The reflection time and activity provided an opportunity for them to begin to receive that "moment", as it is frequently referred to by the

catechists, so as to hold on to and remember it.

4) **Integration:** This, in turn, enabled the experience to be received at a deeper level, intellectually as well as emotionally. A certain "intimacy" was arrived at, and the response was often recorded in affective terms of "enjoying" and savouring the encounter. This resulted in a multiform experience of "connectedness," with God, self, children, and other adults. This integration happens

> "for the soul perceives its own being in the stirrings of the emotions.... Through the emotions, it comes to know what it is and how it is.... They condition that struggle to develop herself to a wholeness and to help others to a corresponding development, which we have found earlier to be characteristic of woman's soul."[118]

5) **Transformation:** The cumulative effect of these interior movements opened the possibility to "meditate" on the experience, to "enter into" it, sometimes to the point of being able to recall it months later. Therefore, these interior movements suggest what Robert Morneau calls "the stirring of the Spirit of God."[119]

> "These stirrings (nudges, impulses, urges, movements, proddings, whispers) cannot be apprehended amidst noise and frenetic activity... Only the grace of tender faith enables us to leap into the mystery.... As that grace is offered and accepted we catch the movements of our God."

New growth gradually appeared; and it was both a growing into it and letting this growth germinate in oneself. To symbolize this growth, the symbols of the seed and leaven were employed earlier. Now these symbols can be expanded, in light of the catechists' images for their personal experience, to include the transformative element. It can be seen in the individual's receiving of what we have called the sources of the encounter with God, scripture and liturgy—symbolized by the seed and leaven. The transformative element is seen also in the quality of the individual's responsiveness.

The simple graph below (Figure 3) is used to show these complementary movements, which reveal an inner view, so to speak, of the transformative element. The *source* is the gift coming from God, especially through biblical and liturgical means. The gift is received into the ground or soil of oneself and germinates there. Through the attentiveness dynamic, it bears fruit in a response. For example, in meditation, as seen in Ruth going over her journal for a few days in the summer; or explicitly in prayer, as seen in Francesca's summer-long journal process. And what is most pronounced in these personal accounts is the clear indication that God, symbolized as sower and seed, is the "Source" of that this transformation.

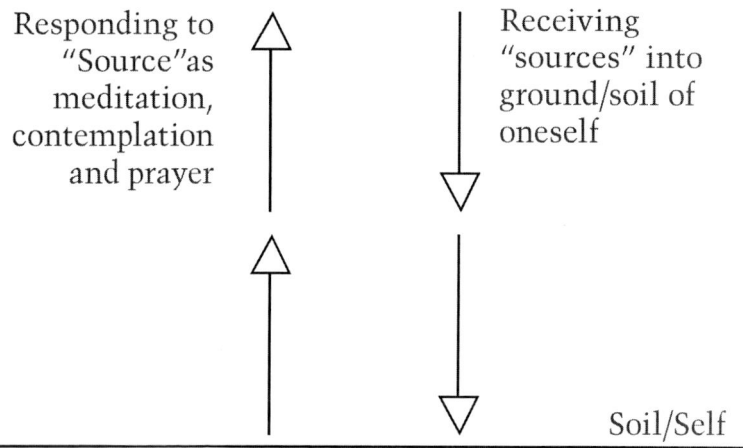

Figure 3

Then we discovered the importance of the children's' presence as an aspect common to all the catechists' experience. This was true even when the catechists were describing their own personal summary of the journey, in which the presence of children would not necessarily be expected to appear. As we mentioned, is very significant that this is a commonality in all the catechists' images. Most especially, it indicates that the catechesis not only enabled them to give to children but also to receive from children. For this reason the presence of children was called "formative" for these catechists.

Above all, the catechists' experience is rooted in God. We recall Domenica's desire to be

> "more appreciative of God, first of all; every time I came to the course I learned how to appreciate and know [that] all the time he is there and to remember he's there...."

Also, it was clear that God is at the heart of all the many levels of relationships which the catechists describe. And so we conclude with this simple diagram (Figure 4). It builds on the former one (Figure 2, chapter 7) and emphasizes God as the source of the whole cycle of relationships. Or, as Domenica puts it, "God, first of all."

Complete Cycle of Relationship

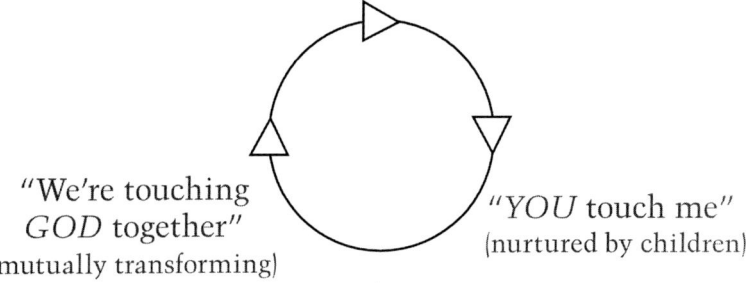

Figure 4

Appendix A:
Letter of Sofia Cavaletti: 2009

A Special *Foglietto* without a Number: April 2009

Why a special, unnumbered *Foglietto*?

Because I would like to ponder again with you the spreading of the Catechesis of the Good Shepherd, a diffusion which, for years, had not ceased to grow and has now reached five continents, always eliciting the same response of joy and enchantment in the little ones and in the older ones.

This is certainly not something new in our reflections.

But something has happened in these days which I want to share with you. Three Missionaries of Charity (Mother Teresa's sisters) came to visit me [..] The Sisters told me that in the general chapter which they had last summer, they decided to adopt the Catechesis of the Good Shepherd, both with children, in transmitting the Judeo-Christian message, and in the formation of their Sisters.

There are approximately 5,000 Missionaries of Charity in the world, and they reach those who, according to the Gospel of Luke, chapter four, are the favored recipients of the Judeo-Christian message, that is, the "poorest," the "least."

When asked: "What have you found in the Catechesis of the Good Shepherd that is different from other catechesis?" they

Appendix A

answered: "contemplation."

In the face of such an affirmation, all words of my own are inadequate. However, I would like to ask you to join me in singing:

> "My soul magnifies the Lord, and
> my spirit exults in God, my Savior."

With much love,

Sofia

Translated by Rebekah Rojcewicz

Appendix B:
Letter of Sofia Cavaletti: 2010

Sofia Cavalletti's Letter of Acceptance of the "St. Catherine of Siena" Award
February 2010

First, I wish to thank all those present who are involved with Aquinas, including its president, the Rev Father Richard Peddicord, for having decided to honor me with the Catherine of Siena Award, even if it has meant overestimating my level of accomplishment.

I would like to begin by speaking of a marvelous adventure that began in 1954 and that bears the name: "the Catechesis of the Good Shepherd." Why do I say "adventure?" An adventure is something that begins and then unfolds in an unexpected way, without our knowing where it will take us, without our having made a program, without equipping ourselves beforehand. In other words, an adventure is a journey we undertake without packing our bags or even having a specific destination.

To give you a sense of the magnitude of the adventure, I would like to offer a statistic. We began with 3 to 5 children. Now, almost every day we receive news of groups beginning the catechesis with children here, there, and everywhere. Plus, an ever growing number of formation courses for catechists. Rather than go on and on, I will simply say that we are now present on 5 continents.

Appendix B

The adventure began with one child—Paolo—whose eyes, after the reading and meditation on the first account of creation in Genesis, filled with tears because he didn't want the session to end. We catechists can say that Paolo showed us the direction of our lives.

Later we began to hear stories of similar responses of the children at the end of the 2-hour atrium session when it was time to go home, and these responses were coming from atria in an ever-increasing variety of socio-economic settings. Thus, we began to wonder, "Who are the children?" What kind of relationship does God have with the human creature in the earliest stage of life?"

In fact, the children involved were younger than 6, the conventional age for beginning religious education, and eventually included children even younger than three years of age.

We found ourselves on a very uncharted path, a path we had not "asked for or ever imagined", because we had not even known it existed. Slowly, slowly, as we inched along, we came to realize that beneath the "dust" on that pathway, a treasure was hidden. *The treasure is the desire of the children to prolong the time of the atrium sessions, the silence they create in the rooms where they do their work, and their manifestations of joy*—a joy that is so different from the "excitement" we usually associate with young children, a joy that renders them deeply satisfied and at peace. (Author's emphasis) It is a joy that seems to be rooted in the deepest part of the person and seems to satisfy the child's deepest, most vital needs, so much so that a child with Downs Syndrome, after a particular atrium presentation and meditation sighed and said, "My body is happy."

With that first group of children in 1954, we had decided to read together the first account of creation in Genesis, a reading that took almost two hours, so that it was then time to go home. But—and this is the beginning of the adventure for us adults—Paolo was there in the group. Paolo was six or seven years old. He had resisted coming that day because it meant giving up the one afternoon he had free during the week. Yet, when the moment came to end the session and go home and not come back for a whole week, his big, black eyes filled with tears.

That small group of five children has multiplied to now "populate" 5 continents where we have witnessed almost the same responses of deep interest in the "good news" that has been chosen and presented to them, and we have observed the same longing in the children to "keep going", because even two whole hours feel "too short."

For all the past 56 years we have been carried along by a question, a question that is deeply embedded in our hearts: "Who are you, child, and how do you live your relationship with God?" It is the question that over these many years has come to be formulated as: "What is the nature of the relationship God has with the human creature in their childhood, especially in the earliest stage of life?"

Gradually over these many years as we have observed the children at work, it has become apparent to us that there are certain "constants" in their interests and responses. In other words, we observed that there were particular materials—handmade, as always, by the catechists and atrium community—which the children regularly chose and with which they seemed never to tire of working, while other catechetical materials languished on the shelves. For the most part, those materials they continuously used focused their attention on themes that

Appendix B

were present in the most ancient tradition of the Church and that constitute the essential points of the Judeo-Christian message, arousing the responses of interest and joy which we have tried here to describe.

It has not been difficult to realize that the essential themes on which the catechesis of the Good Shepherd has come to be based all converge at a central point: the covenant. And thus, these themes represent the very heart of the biblical-liturgical tradition.

This convergence has become apparent beginning with the response of the youngest children to the parable of the Good Shepherd who calls his sheep by name (God initiating the covenant) and the sheep listening to His voice and following him (the creature's response to the covenant). An announcement of this sort creates a bond of love which is so satisfying and enjoyable that 3-year old Mark (Canada), when his mother was putting him to bed and had reminded him that the Good Shepherd knew his name, replied to her, "He doesn't call me Mark; he calls me Joy."

I don't want to detain you too long, but I cannot close without recalling a very beautiful moment in our "adventure": it was the moment when we realized what a marvelous tool the catechesis is in ecumenical relationships (with the Episcopalians, Orthodox Christians, Lutherans and others).

Our formation courses for catechists, regardless of church affiliation, give the same presentations (with only minor adaptations for the differing liturgical prayers) as would be given to an exclusively Catholic group. And this has never created a problem.

Like Leaven

Who knows, perhaps the children have a special future in ecumenism.

Sofia Cavalletti
February 2010
Rome

Translated, and Presented by Rebekah Rojcewicz
Commencement Ceremony, May 7, 2010
Aquinas Institute of Theology
St. Louis, Missouri, USA

Appendix C:
Contemplation and Formation

The Letter

In April 2009 Sofia Cavalletti wrote a brief letter for the international newsletter (*Foglietto*, in Italian). Although it was short—not quite filling one page—she makes an exception in what is the usual content and custom of sending out the newsletter (See Appendix A).

This point already signals something important. Usually the newsletter includes many and various items of interest, and each issue is sent at regular intervals, with a consecutive number. What Sofia is writing about is so relevant and timely that she chooses to send this note on its own without a number, to name it as a "special" issue, and to open with the question: "Why a special, unnumbered *Foglietto*?"

We are told about the visit from three Missionaries of Charity (the community founded Blessed Mother Teresa) that has just happened. Sofia learned that a decision was made the previous summer, during the general gathering of Sisters representing their entire community. They decided "to adopt the Catechesis of the Good Shepherd (CGS), both with children, in transmitting the Judeo-Christian message, and in the formation of their Sisters."

As if this fact were not "special" enough in itself, there is a stand-alone sentence that seems to me to leap off the page: "When the three Sisters are asked: "What have you found in the CGS that is different from other ways of catechesis?" they answered: "contemplation."

Invitations

Then come the closing lines that convey a sort of crescendo effect. Why does Sofia call this one-word response an "affirmation"? What is it about this element of contemplation—which the Sisters identify as *the* defining characteristic of our catechesis—that causes Sofia at this point to abandon words as "inadequate"? Further, there is such a significance in this affirmation about "contemplation" that Sofia is moved to sing, "My soul magnifies the Lord, and my spirit exults in God, my Savior" (Luke 1:46-47).

Even more, there is obviously something here that is intended for us because there is an all-inclusive invitation for the readers to join in Mary's song of praise too. What do you hear that you are being invited into when Sofia asks us to sing the first words of the *Magnificat* together with her?

Each of us hears our own invitations, of course. Considering contemplation in the context of formation, I offer some first thoughts relating to five invitations I hear:

1) to attend
2) to explore
3) to search
4) to dialogue
5) to be open

Appendix C

1) To attend

What does it mean that these three Missionaries of Charity single out contemplation as *the* aspect in the Catechesis of the Good Shepherd (CGS) that differentiates it from all other forms of catechesis? Does this seem a surprising response from Sisters who belong to a congregation recognized by all faiths as one of, if not, the most "active" communities in the world? Is it precisely because they are "contemplatives in action," as Blessed Mother Teresa envisioned the members of the community she founded, that they have attributed priority to contemplation in our catechesis?

The first invitation I hear is to attend to this reality of contemplation in my life. And also to appreciate anew its tremendous value in the formation experiences that I have been privileged to live with children and adults in the Catechesis.

Contemplation certainly has a long and rich role in our Christian tradition, and in the more than 55-year history of the Catechesis of the Good Shepherd. Each of us in this catechesis has our own personal understanding of contemplation with respect to both these traditions.

An article I found helpful as a lens through which to attend to contemplation in my life is called, "Contemplation: A Long Loving Look at the Real."[120] Its author, Walter Burghardt, SJ, delves into each of those four words at length.

2) To explore

Another invitation I hear is to explore the contemplative dynamic underlying our catechesis. Although this is too big a subject to deal with in depth here, let's take the four words in the title of the Burghardt article as a starting point for our conversation, and also as a framework for what follows. Here are just a few references from Sofia's two seminal volumes on *The Religious Potential of the Child* that highlight the resonance between those four words and some essential, and essentially contemplative, elements in our catechesis. These books are referred to below in abbreviated form.[121]

Long:

"We should not be in a hurry; we know the time of the Spirit is slow." (*RP I*, p. 66)

"Before telling me what to do, moral formation must invite and allow me to fall in love; and falling in love takes time." (*RP II*, p. 85)

"We are speaking about moments in which the child seems to be recollected in a kind of spellbound silence as if he or she was trying to protect a fermentation going on deep within." (*RP II*, p. 1)

Loving:

"The religious experience is fundamentally an experience of love and, for the human person, love is essential to life. [We] are not satisfied with merely living, but living as one who is loved and loving." (*RP I*, p. 22)

"In the religious experience [the youngest children] respond with their whole selves and with particular enjoyment. They linger in order to savor the experience with the entirety of their being… The child's contribution in his or her relationship with God is of the highest quality: the enjoyment of the presence of God." (*RP II*, p. 9)

Appendix C

Look:

> "Wonder is a dynamic value; nevertheless it does not drive us to activism but draws us to activity, to an activity we do as persons immersed in the contemplation of something that exceeds us. Maybe the particularity of wonder is that we find activity and contemplation inseparably blended within it." (*RP I*, pp. 138-139)

> "What is needed is an education to covenant… It is the objective and descriptive moment of the reality in which we live. We could call it the "contemplative moment," the moment when reality dawns upon us." (*RP II*, p. 86)

Real:

> "Through signs we become accustomed to search the horizon for a different reality… The encounter with Christ, primordial sign, opens to [us] the infinite space of the transcendent." (*RP I*, pp. 166-167)

> "From objective observation of reality, we enter into a personal relationship with God. The biblical message applies to our most basic human experiences and illuminates those experiences with a message of love and hope." (*RP II*, p. 22)

> "The form of the parable invites ongoing reflection. The child's response of deep satisfaction and joy occurs when the hunger to know the reality in which he or she lives is fed with the Gospel message." (*RP II*, p. 3)

3) To search

A third invitation is to search more closely for the contemplative aspect within our catechesis, and thus to see it as a truly vital dimension in helping children and adults alike to live their religious potential to the full.

There is too much to detail here. I limit myself to a few references from the "The Spirit of the Catechesis: 32 Points of Reflection."[122] Once again, I use schematic form to indicate briefly the primacy that the dynamism of contemplation holds in the catechesis, both explicitly and implicitly. There are two occasions in which the word is used explicitly:

> "The atrium is a community in which children and adults live together a religious experience…a place of prayer, in which work and study spontaneously become meditation, contemplation and prayer." (*RP II*, #3, p. 133)

> "The tasks of the catechist include… preparing an environment and maintaining order in that environment [the atrium] so that it fosters concentration, silence and contemplation in both the child and the adult." (*RP II*, #24, p. 137)

Seen again in the framework of the four words from the above article, here are a few inherently contemplative references, emphasized with italics.

Long:

> "The reasons why the catechist is requested to make the materials with his/her own hands are…*to combat hurry.…*" (*RP II*, #25, p. 137)

Loving:

> "The atrium is a place in which the only Teacher is

Christ; both children and adults place themselves in a *listening stance* before his Word and *seek to penetrate* the mystery of the liturgical celebration." (*RP II, #3,* p. 134)

Look:

"The Catechesis of the Good Shepherd especially honors the spiritual values of childhood and wishes to nurture the *formation of a consciousness....*" (*RP II, #28,* p. 138)

Real:

"The material is placed at the disposal of the child. The children's personal work with the material aids their *meditation and absorption* of the theme presented." (*RP II, #17,* p. 136)

4) To dialogue

The fourth invitation is to engage in conversation together about key components in our catechesis, and to view them as primarily intended to nourish and sustain this contemplative dynamic.

First, it may be helpful to offer a word of background about the long, shared history we have in light of this dynamic. For example, that is exactly the context in which the "32 reflections" came to be written. There was a lengthy and communal process by which they came to birth. In fact, it took three years and involved many persons representing the whole international community.[123] This in itself points to the practical fruitfulness of the CGS's commitment to a contemplative approach.

Even a glance at the title of this little document suggests the contemplative orientation of our catechesis: "The Spirit of the Catechesis: 32 Points of Reflection." There was great intention about this choice of wording, as in every point of reflection. It is also nuanced. For instance, it is interesting to note what these "points" are *not* named (for example, I admit to having called them "guidelines").

I am reminded of the importance that Sofia attributes to the crucial interrelationship between "content" and "method":

> "Therefore the method we use should be one that does not enclose or restrict, one that does not give the impression that everything has already been researched and resolved and that nothing remains for the individual to do."[124]

Using Sofia's metaphor of the butterfly, my understanding of the intention underlying these 32 reflection points is not to codify, much less "pin down" our work, but rather to give it wings: "To explain the parables is like fixing a butterfly on a pin; the wings are still there but the butterfly can no longer fly."[125] That is, this little document is not a point of arrival. Instead, it is intended as a departure point for our own personal reflection and discussion among all of us.

So let's look again briefly at some of the tasks in the Catechesis which do present themselves as "demanding." For instance:

> "...the adult has many demanding tasks to accomplish if [one] wants to help the child live [one's] relationship with God.... The adult should prepare an environment for the child, in the exact sense of a place but also and especially an environment in the wider significance of the word, meaning the community of faith."[126]

And let's try to re-frame some of them by focusing on their

Appendix C

contemplative possibilities. Italics are added in the following few references to emphasize this aspect.

1) Making Material:

"The reasons why the catechist is requested to make the materials with his/her own hands are: *to absorb the content more deeply."* (*RP II*, #25, p. 137)

2) Observation:

"The attitude of the adult has to be marked by humility before the capacities of the child, establishing a right rapport with the child, that is to say, respecting the personality of the child, and *waiting for the child to reveal himself/herself."* (*RP II*, #23, p. 137)

"The catechist observes and studies the vital needs of the child and the *manifestations of those vital needs...."* (*RP II*, #1, p. 133)

3) Creating a Personal Album/Handbook

"The themes...are taken from the Bible and the liturgy (prayers and sacraments) as the fundamental sources for creating and sustaining Christian life *at every developmental stage."* (*RP II*, #5, p. 134)

"The Catechesis of the Good Shepherd is also concerned with helping adults *open their eyes* to the hidden riches of the child, especially to the child's spiritual wealth, so that adults will be *drawn to learn from the child and* to serve him/her." (*RP II*, #27, p. 137)

Could a contemplative re-framing of these tasks bring balance to what can appear mostly as obligations? Would an attempt to shift the focus a little help them to be received mainly as opportunities? By that I mean, opportunities to grow in our own contemplative potential, as well as to help the child's relationship with God; opportunities to feed our awareness of how formative, even transformative, the child's presence can be in *our* covenant relationship with God.

5) To be open

The fifth invitation is a willingness to be open to new horizons in our catechesis as a contemplative adventure, as this reflection point seems to indicate:

> "The Catechesis of the Good Shepherd has an experimental character and is *open to go always deeper into the infinite mystery* of God and God's cosmic covenant with God's creatures." (*RP II, #32*, p. 138)

I end these initial thoughts by sharing an "experiment" that emerged as part of a pastoral research process I was grateful to engage in with seven catechists. All the persons in this process had experience in the catechesis, from a few years to almost a dozen. Each person was given sheets with evocative questions, and invited to reflect on them directly after:

A) their experience of the second level course (see the first box below);

B) their experience in their second level atrium), including the children's first Communion and Reconciliation retreat (see the second box below).

Why such simple reflection points? These few words of Sofia, that follow each box below, flesh out the purpose behind them.

Appendix C

Adult Session: Reflections   **Date**
What topic/theme was presented in this seminar?
In what way was I touched by it? And why?

"It is only through a continued and profound observation of reality that we become conscious of its many aspects, of the secrets and mysteries it contains. Openness to reality and openness to wonder proceed at the same pace. As we gradually enter into what is real, our eyes will come to see it as more and more charged with marvels and wonder will become a habit of our spirit." (*RP I*, p. 139)

Children's Session: Observations   **Date**
In attending to the children, what did you notice…see… hear…and so forth?

"…the child becomes a teacher of the spiritual life, the bearer of a jubilant message, proclaimed through his or her relationship with God." (*RP II*, p. 25)

"The contemplative nature of the children is particularly evidenced during the retreat. We get to witness an aspect of their contemplative nature… For the catechists, the first Communion retreat is a profound experience of witnessing the mysterious bond between God and his smallest creatures and the unique rhythm of their life together." (*RP II*, p. 107)

It seemed to be fruitful for all the catechists to allow a brief time, even if only 15 minutes, for the above reflections, after the course and atrium sessions.

But with the ever-increasing items on our "to do" lists, doesn't it seem just too much of a "luxury" to take the time, however brief, for contemplative practices like these, or others to which the Holy Spirit might be inclining each of us? The contemplative thrust embedded in the CGS is undeniably challenging. It may be one of its most radically counter-cultural aspects. "Just do it," is a slogan that our society—Canadian and American at least—emulates, and literally "buys into;" "getting it done" is awarded its highest affirmation.

All the same, the final sentence in Walter Burghardt's article contains an invitation that touches upon what seems to me the soul of our catechesis: "Contemplation, my friends, is not a luxury; it is the mark of a lover; it is the mark of a Christian."[127]

Patricia Coulter
Summer, 2009.

Endnotes

Introduction

1. Barbara Schmich Searle, "A Celebration of the Life of Tina Lillig" (*Journal of the Catechesis of the Good Shepherd*, No, 26, 2011), p. 5-9.

Chapter One: Telling the Stories

2. Gabrielle Roy, *The Hidden Mountain*. Trans. Henry Binsse. (Toronto: McClelland and Stewart Limited, 1975), p. 123. The phrase, "To tell my story" is taken from *Hamlet*, by William Shakespeare.

3. *Ibid*, p. 89; p. 109. "And yet it was a very simple little thing", p. 108.

4. *Ibid.*, p. 109.

5. *Ibid.*, p. 123.

6. Maria Montessori, "How It All Happened," (*Association Montessori Internationale Communications*, No. 2/3, 1970), p. 5-6. Dr. Silvana Montanaro outlined Montessori's works in religious education in her article, "Maria Montessori and the Religious Education of the Child" (*Journals of the Catechesis of the Good Shepherd*: 1984-1997, Dec. 1990), p. 177-178.

7. See: Sofia's chapter (10) in *The Child in the Church, Maria Montessori and Others*. Ed. E.M. Standing (St. Paul, MN: Catechetical Guild, 1965). Sofia clearly notes this contribution in this early presentation of the beginnings of their work. For instance, see p. 132. Henceforward this volume will be referred to as *The Child in the Church*.

8. Sofia Cavalletti, "Symposium- Amsterdam, 25.4.1984" (*Association Montessori International Communications*, No.2/3, 1984), p.13.

9. Sofia Cavalletti, *The Religious Potential of the Child: Experiencing*

Scripture and Liturgy with Young Children. Trans. Julie M. Coulter and Patricia M. Coulter. (Chicago: Liturgy Training Publications, 1992) p. 158. Henceforward this volume will be referred to as *Religious Potential I*.

10. *On Catechesis In Our Time* (*Catechesi Tradendae*), 1.5.

11. Sofia Cavalletti, "The Characteristics of Catechists of the Good Shepherd" (*Journals of the Catechesis of the Good Shepherd* 1984-1997, Spring, 1986), p. 60.

12. Sr. Elaine McCarron, "Catechetical Sunday—Then and Now" (*Currents, NCCB/USCC*, Sept. 1995), p.3.

13. See "The Spirit of the Catechesis: 32 Points of Reflection," Appendix 1, *The Religious Potential of the Child 6 to 12 Years Old.* Trans. Rebekah Rojcewicz and Alan Perry (Chicago: Liturgy Training Publications, 2002) p.138. Henceforward referred to as *Religious Potential II*.

14. See "Notes for Catechists and Curriculum for Children" in Appendix B, *The Good Shepherd and The Child: A Joyful Journey*, Sofia Cavalletti, Patricia Coulter, Gianna Gobbi, Silvana Quattrocchi Montanaro, M.D., and Rebekah Rojcewicz (Chicago: Liturgy Training Publications, 2014), p. 96. Henceforward referred to as *Joyful Journey*.

Chapter Two: Adults: Seven Companions

15. *Guide for Catechists: Document of vocational, formative, and promotional orientation of Catechists in the territories dependent on the Congregation for the Evangelization of Peoples*, Part 1, No. 2 (Congregation for the Evangelization of Peoples, Vatican City, 1993), p. 9.

16. Gianna Gobbi, *Listening to God with Children: The Montessori Method Applied to the Catechesis of Children.* Translator/editor: Rebekah Rojcewicz (Ohio: Treehaus, 1998), p. 4. Henceforward referred to as *Listening to God with Children*.

17. Gianna Gobbi, "Practical Suggestions," *Joyful Journey*, p. 30.

18. Chapter 4: "An Adventure: The Catechesis of the Good Shepherd", *Way of Holy Joy: Selected Writings of Sofia Cavalletti* (Chicago, Il: Liturgy

Training Publications, 2012), p. 39-40. Henceforward referred to as *Way of Holy Joy.*

19. Barbara Matera, "A Glimpse into an Atrium" (*Pastoral Liturgy*, May/June 2012, Volume 43, Number 3), p. 11.

20. Gretchen Wolff Pritchard, "Onward and Upward With the Good Shepherd" (*The Sunday Paper: Materials For Christian Education, Epiphany*, 1996), p. 2.

21. Robert Holton, "Holy Things" (*Our Sunday Visitor*, April 14, 1996), p. 12.

22. *Adult Catechesis in the Christian Community: Some Principles and Guidelines: With Discussion Guide*, International Council For Catechesis, 1990. (Washington, DC: United States Catholic Conference, 1992, No. 56), p.26.

23. Kate Convissor, "Feed My Lambs" (*St. Anthony Messenger*, Vol. 101/No. 3, August 1993), p. 21.

24. *Ibid.*, p. 20.

25. *Adult Catechesis in the Christian Community*, No. 76, p, 31.

26. Mark Searle, as quoted in Kate Convissor's article, "Feed My Lambs," p. 19.

27. Kate Convissor, "Feed My Lambs," p. 19.

28. See the Foreword in *Joyful Journey* by Archbishop Marcel Gervais, Ottawa, Canada, p. V.

29. Elizabeth McMahon Jeep, "A Very Fragile Treasure: A New Look at Ministry to Children" (*Church*, Fall, 1993, Volume 9, Number 3), p. 48.

Chapter Three: Children: A "Different Way of Being Christians"

30. Charles Péguy, "Innocence and Experience", *Basic Verities: Prose and Poetry*. Rendered into English by Ann and Julian Green. (New York:

Books for Libraries Press, 1972), p. 227.

31. Maria Montessori, "On Religious Education" (Course Lecture, London, 1946), *The Child, Society and the World: Unpublished Speeches and Writings* (The Clio Montessori Series, Volume 7), p.40.

32. Edward Robinson, *The Original Vision: A Study of the Religious Experience of Childhood* (New York: The Seabury Press, 1983), p. 7-8.

33. Sofia Cavalletti, Chapter 5: "My Readings", *Way of Holy Joy*, p. 68.

34. Gilbert Keith Chesterton, "A Defence of Baby-Worship", *The Defendant* (London: J.M. Dent & Sons Ltd., 1947), p. 149.

35. Sofia Cavalletti, *Joyful Journey*. p. 9.

36. *Ibid.*, p. 12.

37. C.S. Lewis, "The Weight of Glory", in *The Weight of Glory and Other Addresses* (New York: Harper One, 2001) p. 18-19.

38. Maria Montessori, "God and the Child," in *The Child in the Church*, p. 16 ff.

39. Rev. Thomas Keating, *Intimacy with God* (New York: Crossroad, 1995), p.22.

40. Sofia Cavalletti, *Joyful Journey*, p. 12.

41. *Ibid.*, p. 13.

42. *Ibid.*, p. 9. This is one of the many points of connection between the Montessori approach and this catechesis, which I highlighted in schematic form in the reflection, "The Spirituality of Childhood" (*Journals of the Catechesis of the Good Shepherd* 1998-2002), p. 118-9.

43. Sofia Cavalletti, "On Moral Formation" (*Journals of the Catechesis of the Good Shepherd* 1984-1997, Fall 1988), p. 133.

44. Sofia Cavalletti, Chapter 4, "An Adventure: The Catechesis of the Good Shepherd," *Way of Holy Joy*, p. 34.

45. *Ibid.*, p. 33.

Endnotes

46. Sofia Cavalletti, "The Receivers of the Proclamation," *Religious Potential I*, p. 49. Obviously, this is also a core theme in Gianna Gobbi's work *Listening to God with Children*.

47. Sofia Cavalletti, Chapter 10, *Religious Potential I*, p. 159. Dr. Montessori also states that she found her "pedagogical technique" (technique pédagogique) in the liturgy itself, and she sought to "open" the liturgy (the Eucharist particularly) by opening "the book" (of Scripture, and the Roman Missal, in use at the time). For example, see *L'Education Religieuse: La Vie En Jésus-Christ*. Trans. Georgette J.-J. Bernard et Anne-Marie Bernard. (Paris: Desclée de Brouwer, 1956), p. 19ff; 136-37.

48. Thomas Groome, *Sharing Faith: A Comprehensive Approach to Religious Education and Pastoral Ministry: The Way of Shared Praxis* (San Francisco: Harper Collins, 1991), p. 156-57. Groome is quoting from Sofia's *Religious Potential I*, p. 98.

49. For example, see Sofia Cavalletti, *The Religious Potential of the Child, Vol. II*: "The child brings to the relationship all the dignity of a true partner," p. 8.

50. Sofia Cavalletti, *Joyful Journey*, p. 12.

51. Maria Montessori, "On Religious Education," (Course Lecture, London, 1946), *The Child, Society and the World: Unpublished Speeches and Writings* (The Clio Montessori Series, Volume 7), p. 38.

52. Sofia Cavalletti, "Religious Formation and Later Childhood" (*Journals of the Catechesis of the Good Shepherd*, 1984-1997), p. 4. See *Religious Potential II*, p. 25.

53. Sofia Cavalletti, *Religious Potential II*. p. 84.

Chapter Four: Being in Love

54. Sofia Cavalletti, *Joyful Journey*, p. 94.

55. Bernard Lonergan S.J., *Method in Theology* (New York: The Seabury Press, 1973), p. 105; 122. The horizontal dimension is also implied in this, which, according to Avery Dulles, is the "mystical communion"

ecclesiology, that is, "the People of God of the New Covenant." *Models of the Church* (Garden City, New York: Doubleday/Image Books, 1978), p. 58.

56. Sofia Cavalletti, *Religious Potential II*, p. 85.

57. Sofia Cavalletti, *Joyful Journey*, p. 57.

58. Maria Montessori, *The Child in the Church*, p. 16.

59. Sofia Cavalletti, *A Joyful Journey*, p. 13.

60. Sofia Cavalletti, *The Religious Potential of the Child, Vol. II*, p. 85.

61. Maria Montessori, *The Child in the Church*, p. 15.

62. Karl Rahner, "Ideas for a Theology of Childhood", *Theological Investigations*, Volume VIII, pp. 33-50. Trans. David Bourke. (New York: Herder and Herder, 1971), p. 33. This essay is also treated in Ann M. Garrido's *Mustard Seed Preaching* (Chicago, IL.: Liturgy Training Publications, 2004).

63. *Ibid.*, p. 36.

64. *Ibid.*, p. 37.

65. Maria Montessori, *The Child in the Church*, p. 15-16.

66. Karl Rahner, "Ideas for a Theology of Childhood," p. 41.

67. *Ibid.*, p. 34:

68. Sofia Cavalletti, Chapter 2, "The Child as Parable," *Way of Holy Joy.*

69. Hans-Ruedi Weber, *Jesus and the Children: Biblical Resource for Study and Preaching* (Geneva: World Council of Churches, 1979), p. viii.

70. Sofia Cavalletti, Chapter 2, *Way of Holy Joy*, p. 13.

71. *Ibid.*, p.15.

72. *Ibid.*, p. 16; 18.

Endnotes

73. *Ibid.*, p. 15.

Chapter Five: The the Sources

74. As indicated here and in earlier accounts, in excerpting the catechists' journals every attempt has been made to reproduce the author's emphasis as closely as possible. Although this results in some particularities of style (e.g., arrows, brackets, underscoring, etc.), these have been retained to convey the individuality of their handwritten accounts.

75. "Resta Con Noi, Signore, La Sera", *La Famiglia Cristiana nella Casa del Padre: Repertorio di canti per la liturgia* (Torino: Elle Di Ci, 2005), p. 330. This experience of joy is of such significance to Domenica that it recurs in her accounts, and thus will be referred to in later chapters as well. The "joy" Domenica associates with this song recalls this line from St. Augustine: "A song is a thing of joy and, if we think carefully about it, a thing of love". Sermon 34, 1-3, *The Divine Office: Liturgy of the Hours According to the Roman Rite* (Dublin: Talbot Press, 1974), p. 537.

76. As a general guide to this and following chapters, especially for those who may be new to this catechesis, the source of the theme to which the catechist is specifically referring will be noted. For example, for future references to the True Vine parable, see: Sofia Cavalletti, Ch. 7, "The Covenant in the Parables," *Religious Potential II.* See also: Sofia Cavalletti, Ch. 4, "The Parable of the True Vine in the Gospel according to John", *Ways to Nurture the Relationship with God.*

77. Mary is referring to what is called the "maxim" material: certain sayings of Jesus in the Gospel are singled out and written on individual wooden tablets for the children's use. For future references to the material for these maxims, see Sofia Cavalletti, Ch. 11, "Our Living of History", *Religious Potential II.*

78. For future references to the timeline spoken of here on the "Unity of the History of the Kingdom of God," see Ch. 3, "The Globality of Biblical History," *Religious Potential II.*

79. In the sessions on the Eucharistic rite, the core themes were presented

as they are to children: each element is individualized (e.g., what are referred to in this catechesis as "the gestures of gift") and presented in terms of its liturgical movement as well as its accompanying prayer. For future references to these Eucharistic gestures, see Ch. 13, "Moral Life and Liturgy: Part II: The Eucharist," *Religious Potential II*.

80. For future references to the theme and presentation of the part of the Eucharistic rite which is called the "Mystery of Faith," see Ch. 9, "Our Living of History, Part I: Liturgy and the Mystery of Faith," *Religious Potential II*.

81. Eileen refers here to the unpublished reflection offered by the late Fr. Mongillo on "Moral Formation and Reconciliation" during the first International Conference of the CGS (October 19, 1993, Rome). Fr. Mongillo, was a professor of moral theology at the Thomas Aquinas Pontifical Institute (Angelicum) in Rome. His influence on the catechesis is enduring. For example, Sofia acknowledges, in referring to his contribution to the development of the moral aspects of the Catechesis of the Good Shepherd: "I am most indebted to Father Dalmazio Mongillo, OP, and the wisdom he has shared through numerous courses, conferences, seminars and conversations" (*Religious Potential II*, Note 1, p. 95-96). See also Sofia's acknowledgment of Fr. Mongillo in Chapter 5, "My Readings," *Way of Holy Joy*, p. 71-2; and in her article, "Christianity? To Enjoy a Person" (*Journals of the Catechesis of the Good Shepherd 2003-2008*), p.113-115.

82. The "Synthesis of the Mass" is the title of a presentation given to older children, which recapitulates previous Eucharistic themes already offered to them before six years of age in the atrium. The materials consist of models of the sacred vessels (e.g., paten, chalice), and cards for the various gestures (e.g., symbol of hands in various positions to represent the epiclesis, offering, exchange of peace) and prayers (e.g., "Amen"). Accompanying these are other cards that assist in the child's work with this material. For future references to this theme, see Ch. 10, "Our Living of History, Part II: Liturgy: The Sacrament of Cosmic Unity," *Religious Potential II*.

83. Wendy refers here to another core text by Sofia Cavalletti. Originally titled, *Living Liturgy: Elementary Reflections*, Sofia revised it as: *The History of the Kingdom of God, Part 2: Liturgy and the Building of the*

Endnotes

Kingdom of God. Trans. Patricia Coulter, Julie Coulter-English, and Rebekah Rojcewicz. (Chicago: Liturgy Training Publications, 2013). Henceforward this work will be referred to as *HKG, Part 2, Liturgy.* Here, in Part 2, Sofia explains that this work is re-titled to indicate that it is the second part of two volumes that "are, in actuality, one single introduction to the history of the Kingdom of God in its two inseparable components: The Bible and the liturgy." p. xiii. The first volume, on the Bible, is titled *The History of the Kingdom of God, Part 1: From Creation to Parousia.* (Chicago: Liturgy Training Publications, 2012).

Chapter Six: Good News of Great Joy: The Christian Message

84. Another helpful source of information about all the materials mentioned in this work can be found in the series of DVDs of Sofia and Gianna's atrium in Rome. The second DVD specifically addresses the age group treated here, *The Atrium of the Middle Children* and the book entitled, *The Development of the Catechesis of the Good Shepherd: Inside the Atria in Rome.* (Chicago: Liturgy Training Publications, 2014) (available from the National Association of the Catechesis of the Good Shepherd United States, cgsusa.org).

85. Domenica refers here to the series of presentations of the True Vine parable offered to the children during the weeks preceding the celebration of the sacraments of First Eucharist and Reconciliation. This is addressed in the abovementioned DVD, as well as in the earlier references made to the True Vine parable in *Religious Potential II* and *Ways to Nurture the Relationship with God.*

86. For information about this and future references to the sacrament of Reconciliation, see Ch. 12, "Moral Life and Liturgy, Part I: The Sacrament of Reconciliation," *Religious Potential II.*

87. For a profound reflection on the prayer-word "Amen", see *Religious Potential II*, p. 115-16.

88. See Sofia's use of this image of breathing: "the entire universe lives… in a process of cosmic breathing," in *Religious Potential II* (p. 121-22).

See also: "We can consider liturgy to be the breath of the Body of Christ", in *HKG*, Part 2, *Liturgy*, p. 19 and following.

Chapter Seven: The Formative Presence of Children

89. I am indebted to Sofia for the title of this chapter; after reading this work in its earlier form, she remarked that it indicated "the formative presence of children" in the adults' lives.

90. These biblical-liturgical materials, as has already been seen, also engage the adult in a meditative way. This is one of the reasons why catechists are encouraged to be involved in material-making. As Gianna Gobbi states explicitly: "Making the materials by hand is an essential way of entering more deeply into the theme we will present to the children. It helps us to slow down and to pace ourselves more to the rhythm of the child, as well as to be more attentive to the Holy Spirit. Furthermore, material-making is an invaluable opportunity for us as adults to experience the integration of hand, mind and heart," *Listening to God with Children*, p. 28-29.

Chapter Eight: Dynamics of Relationship

91. I am indebted to the work of Henri J. M. Nouwen, *With Burning Hearts: A Meditation on the Eucharistic Life* (Maryknoll, New York: Orbis Books, 1994). Reading his description of this dynamic in the spiritual life helped to articulate what was being discerned in the catechists' accounts; for example, see p. 87. Further references to this work will be made in following chapters as well.

92. This insight recalls a central point repeated by the psychiatrist Dr. Scott M. Peck:" We all have this unrealistic sense of our unimportance, of our unloveliness.... So, I repeat, there is nothing that holds us back more from mental health, from health as a society, and from God than the sense we all have of our own unimportance...." *Further Along the Road Less Travelled: The Unending Journey Toward Spiritual Growth: The Edited Lectures* (New York: Simon & Shuster, 1993), p. 98 and following.

Endnotes

93. *Ecclesia in America*: the full title of this post-synodal document in English is: "On the Encounter with the Living Jesus Christ: The Way to Conversion, Communion and Solidarity in America" (January 22, 1999).

94. "The process of letting go—and of letting come..." is identified as an important spiritual dynamic by W. Grant, Harold Thompson, Mary Magdala, and Thomas Clarke, in From *Image to Likeness: A Jungian Path in the Gospel Journey* (New York: Paulist Press, 1983), p.195-6.

95. Ruth is referring to certain resources that were handed out in relation to the celebration of the sacraments during the First Eucharist retreat. For example, Sofia's article "O Taste and See That the Lord is Good" (*Journals of the Catechesis of the Good Shepherd*, 1984-1997, Spring, 1994), p. 234-236.

Chapter Nine: Ways of Accompaniment

96. Simone Weil, "Reflections on the Right Use of School Studies With a View to the Love of God," *Waiting On God*. Trans. Emma Crauford. (Glasgow: Wm. Collins Sons & Co., 1978), p. 66-76.

97. Thomas Merton, *New Seeds of Contemplation* (New York: A New Directions Book, 1962), p. 32-33.

98. Anne Morrow Lindbergh, *Gift from the Sea* (New York: Signet Books, 1957), p. 54-5.

99. Sofia Cavalletti, *Way of Holy Joy*, p. 15; see also p. 19.

100. Maria Montessori, *The Child in the Church*, p.14

101. Sofia Cavalletti, *Joyful Journey*, p. 13.

102. Sofia Cavalletti, *Religious Potential I*, p.170.

103. Josef Pieper, *Leisure: The Basis of Culture*. Trans. Alexander Dru. (Mentor-Omega Book, 1963), p.24-25.

104. Pam Moore, *Taste and See: Savoring the Child's Wisdom* (Chicago: Liturgy Training Publications, 2011), p. 1X.

105. Maria Montessori, *To Educate the Human Potential* (Madras, India:

Kalakshetra Publications, 1973), p. 121-22.

106. Sofia ascribes great value to this contemplative dimension. For example, see Appendix A. For an early appreciation of this dimension with respect to this catechesis, see Barry C. Miller, "The Contemplative Potential of the Child" (*Professional Approaches for Christian Educators*, No. 23, December 1993), p.15-19.

107. To "be attentive" is the first of what Bernard Lonergan calls the "transcendental precepts," *Method in Theology*, p.20; p. 54.

108. Dolores R. Leckey, "Children in Jeopardy: Who Cares?" (*Church*, Spring 1995), p. 8.

109. Sofia Cavalletti, "Characteristics of the Good Shepherd Catechesis" (*Journals of the Catechesis of the Good Shepherd* 1984-1997, Winter 1985), p. 25. See also Sofia's article "Christianity? To Enjoy a Person" (*Journals of the Catechesis of the Good Shepherd* 2003-2008), p.113-115.

Chapter Ten: Journey Together

110. This chart singles out the presence of children in the catechists' images, as well as various biblical references contained therein. Additionally, other biblical associations are included, which represents a liberty I have taken in considering their accounts as a whole (e.g., as in Francesca's image).

111. Kate's image in this section alludes to the passage from the book of Wisdom noted at the start of this chapter.

112. Henri Nouwen, *With Burning Hearts*, p. 85.

113. Nouwen highlights the significance of not overlooking this aspect of growth that community provides: "I am deeply aware of my own tendency to want to go from communion to ministry without forming community." *Ibid.*, p. 87.

114. Henri Nouwen, p. 87. See also *The Church in America* (*Ecclesia in America*), No. 35.

115. Sofia Cavalletti, "The Characteristics of the Catechists of the Good

Endnotes

Shepherd" (*Journals of the Catechesis of the Good Shepherd* 1984-1997, Spring 1986), p.60.

Epilogue

116. Gerald May, "To Bear the Beams of Love: Contemplation and Personal Growth" (*The Way*, Supplement 59, Summer 1987), p. 26.

117. Edith Stein (Saint Teresa Benedicta of the Cross), "Spirituality of the Christian Woman," *The Collected Works of Edith Stein*, Volume Two. Chapter III, "Essays on Woman." Trans. Freda Mary Oben. (Washington, D.C., ICS Publications, 1987), p. 99.

118. *Ibid.*, p. 96.

119. Bishop Robert F. Morneau, *Mantras From a Poet: Jessica Powers* (Kansas City, MO., Sheed and Ward, 1991), p. 77.

Appendix C: Contemplation and Formation

120. Walter J. Burghardt, S.J., "Contemplation. A Long Loving Look at the Real" (*Church*, Winter, 1989), p.14-18.

121. Sofia Cavalletti, *Religious Potential I* (referred to throughout as *RP I*). Sofia Cavalletti, *Religious Potential II* (referred to throughout as *RP II*).

122. "The Spirit of the Catechesis: 32 Points of Reflection," Appendix I, *R.P. II*, p. 133-38.

123. *Ibid.*, See the note at the conclusion of the abovementioned Appendix I, that begins: "The first draft of these points was done by the Roman Association, May 1993...".

124. Sofia Cavalletti, *R.P. I*, p. 159. Here Sofia is referring specifically to the parables. This holds true, I think, for this approach in general since Sofia also refers to the whole Catechesis as a "parable method."

125. *Ibid.*, p. 162.

126. *Ibid.*, p. 59.

127. W. J. Burghardt, p. 18.

Acknowledgments

With great gratitude to the many persons who contributed in various ways to make this work possible, some of whom have now gone before us "in the hope of the resurrection":

Aloysius Cardinal Ambrozic; Rev. Elliott Allen; Sr. Anne Anderson; Sr. Joan Atkinson; Rev. Ron Barnes; Msgr. Samuel Bianco; Margaret Brennan; Deacon Bert Cambre; Sofia Cavalletti; Yee-ling Chang; Michael Clark; Tilde Cocchini and family; Maria Christlieb; Lesley Critton; Susanna De Angelis; Monica Donnelly; Sr. Rosellla Dowling; Sheila Doyle; Rev. Ralph Eibner; Christine Ennis; Kathleen Ennis; Brother Ignatius Feaver and the Capuchin province of Mary, Mother of the Good Shepherd; David Finnegan; Sr. Cathleen Flynn; Anke Foller-Carroll; Patricia Foley; Ann Garrido; Tarcia Gerwing; Gianna Gobbi; Flaminia Guidi; Mary P. Hayes; Rev. Frank Kelly; Haley Kermis; Elly Kaas; Barbara Kahn; Linda Kaiel; Ed Krupica; Sr. Mary Carol Lemire; Sr. Ellen Leonard; Vivian Ligo; Valentina Lillig; Sr. Kathleen Lyons; Ellen Marchildon; Mimi Marrocco; Karen Maxwell; Elizabeth McCabe; Sr. Elaine McCarron; Rev. Thomas McKillop; Most Reverend Attila Mikloshazy; Deacon Stephen Miletic; Mary Mirrione; Rev. Dalmazio Mongillo; Silvana Quattrocchi Montanaro; Renilde Montessori; Susan Morgan; Catherine Mulroney; Mary-Rose O'Driscoll; Margaret O'Gara; Susan Perna; Rebekah Rojcewicz; Susan Rosgen; Helene Royes; Suzanne Scorsone; Sr. Mary Ellen Sheehan; Rosemary Simmons; Joseph Tanel; William Targett; Brenda Voisin; Sr. Olga Warnke; Ann Marie White; Anne Wiley; Nancy Wood.

My beloved family in all its generations, especially my parents, and sisters Felicity and Christina.

About the Author

Patricia Coulter, D. Min., received her AMI Montessori training in Dublin, Ireland; her formation in the Good Shepherd Catechesis under the guidance of Sofia Cavalletti, Gianna Gobbi, and their colleagues at the Good Shepherd Catechesis Center in Rome; and her undergraduate and graduate degrees at the University of St. Michael's College, University of Toronto.

Throughout their long friendship, Patricia has collaborated with Sofia and Gianna in various course initiatives, translations, and books (*The Good Shepherd and The Child: A Joyful Journey; Ways to Nurture the Relationship with God; Way of Holy Joy: Selected Writings of Sofia Cavalletti*). She has over 30 years' experience with adults and children in the Good Shepherd catechesis, and presently serves as Senior Consultant for Spiritual Formation, Office of Formation for Discipleship, Archdiocese of Toronto.

In 2004, Dr. Coulter was the recipient of the *Pro Ecclesia et Pontifice* cross for her ministry with children and adults.

Photographs

Taken in the Good Shepherd Center of Catechesis, Rome, Italy

Photo 1. Sofia Cavalletti with children working with the timeline material for: The Unity of the History of the Kingdom of God (the moment of the "Parousia").

Photo 2. Gianna Gobbi and children working with the material for the city of Jerusalem.

Photo 3. Maria, almost 3, Bambino Gesu Children's hospital, Rome (Chapter One).

Photo 4. Gianna working on material-making in the atrium.

Photo 5. Prayer table in the atrium with Good Shepherd parable text and statue.

Photo 6. Girl at the cabinet containing the four volumes of the little Gospel books (i.e., the infancy and paschal narratives, parables and miracles).

Photo 7. Boy working with the materials for the maxims (i.e., the evangelical sayings of Jesus).

Photographs

Photo 8. Gianna working with a child in the atrium.

Photo 9: Boy working with a material on the various parts of the rite of the Eucharist.

Photo 10. Children working with the timeline material: The Unity of the History of the Kingdom of God (the moment of "Creation").

Child's Drawing. Monica (8 years old, Canada): detail from her drawing during her First Eucharist Retreat in the atrium.